Information to Support Monitoring and Habitat Restoration on Ash Meadows National Wildlife Refuge

By G. Gary Scoppettone, Editor

Open-File Report 2013-1022

U.S. Department of the Interior
U.S. Geological Survey

U.S. Department of the Interior
KEN SALAZAR, Secretary

U.S. Geological Survey
Marcia K. McNutt, Director

U.S. Geological Survey, Reston, Virginia: 2013

For more information on the USGS—the Federal source for science about the Earth,
its natural and living resources, natural hazards, and the environment—visit
http://www.usgs.gov or call 1–888–ASK–USGS

For an overview of USGS information products, including maps, imagery, and publications,
visit *http://www.usgs.gov/pubprod*

To order this and other USGS information products, visit *http://store.usgs.gov*

Suggested citation:
Scoppettone, G.G., ed., 2013, Information to support to monitoring and habitat restoration on Ash
Meadows National Wildlife Refuge: U.S. Geological Survey Open-File Report 2013-1022, 56 p.

Prologue

The Ash Meadows National Wildlife Refuge staff focuses on improving habitat for the highest incidence of endemic species for an area of its size in the continental United States. Attempts are being made to restore habitat to some semblance of its pre-anthropogenic undisturbed condition, and to provide habitat conditions to which native plant and animal species have evolved. Unfortunately, restoring the Ash Meadows' Oases to its pre-anthropogenic undisturbed condition is almost impossible. First, there are constraints on water manipulation because there are private holdings within the refuge boundary; second, there has been at least one species extinction—the Ash Meadows pool fish (*Empetrichthys merriami*). It is also quite possible that thermal endemic invertebrate species were lost before ever being described. Perhaps the primary obstacle to restoring Ash Meadows to its pre-anthropogenic undisturbed conditions is the presence of invasive species. However, invasive species, such as red swamp crayfish (*Procambarus clarki)* and western mosquitofish (*Gambusia affinis),* are a primary driving force in restoring Ash Meadows' spring systems, because under certain habitat conditions they can all but replace native species. Returning Ash Meadows' physical landscape to some semblance of its pre-anthropogenic undisturbed condition through natural processes may take decades. Meanwhile, the natural dissolution of concrete and earthen irrigation channels threatens to allow cattail marshes to flourish instead of spring-brooks immediately downstream of spring discharge. This successional stage favors non-native crayfish and mosquitofish over the native Amargosa pupfish (*Cyprinodon nevadensis*). Thus, restoration is needed to control non-natives and to promote native species, and without such intervention the probability of native fish reduction or loss, is anticipated.

The four studies in this report are intended to provide information for restoring native fish habitat and for monitoring native fish populations in relation to restoration efforts on the Ash Meadows National Wildlife Refuge. There are no precise records on conditions of each of the spring systems prior to anthropogenic alteration; however, fostering conditions that favor native over non-natives will be key to habitat restoration. Information regarding native species carbon source is needed to create habitat that favors native species, thus habitat restoration fostering food stuff consumed by native species should be considered in restoration efforts. In compiling data for the first part of this report, we tracked carbon source for native and non-native species at four stations along the Jackrabbit Spring system. Thus, we were able to contrast carbon source in warm- and cool-water habitats. Habitat in Jackrabbit Spring was improved for native fishes in 2007. The second paper in this report focuses on native fish populations in Jackrabbit Spring system pre- and post-restoration.

Much of the Ash Meadows Oases is marsh habitat where non-native red swamp crayfish and western mosquitofish are often abundant, to the detriment of non-natives. Because marsh habitat is broadly represented in the Ash Meadows landscape, establishing marsh habitat most conducive to the native fishes is important to the restoration effort, and the third paper addresses marsh habitat type with the relative abundance of fishes and crayfish.

There are previous years of monitoring Ash Meadows' native fish populations, but not all monitoring occurred at the same time of year. Desert-fish populations sometimes undergo seasonal fluctuation, so it might not be valid to compare population trends using different seasons. For report four, we tracked a closed population of Amargosa pupfish (*Cyprinodon nevadensis*) year round to track seasonal trends. Knowledge of seasonal trends is important in tracking changes of populations pre- and post-restoration.

Contents

Figures

Tables

Information to Support Monitoring and Habitat Restoration on Ash Meadows National Wildlife Refuge

By G. Gary Scoppettone, Editor

Carbon Source and Trophic Structure of Fishes and Crayfish along the Jackrabbit Spring System, and Implications for Habitat Restoration

By G. Gary Scoppettone, Danielle Johnson, J. Antonio Salgado, Peter H. Rissler, and Mark Hereford, U.S. Geological Survey; and Michael S. Parker, Southern Oregon University

Restoration of Ash Meadows Spring systems aimed at enhancing habitat for native fishes requires understanding the spring ecosystems' primary energy source, because habitat manipulation should target enhancement of energy flow to the native fishes. In thermal springs, such as those in Ash Meadows, water cools in a downstream direction (Garside and Schilling, 1979); how the flow of energy may differ for native and non-native species in the warmer stream reach compared to the cooler reach is unknown. How native fishes overlap in food resources with non-native species in warm-water as opposed to cool-water habitats also is unknown.

Investigation of carbon sources and trophic position of fishes and crayfish in the Jackrabbit Spring system can provide useful information for future Ash Meadows restoration projects and the ongoing management of the restored systems. In this study, we compare carbon source and trophic position in warm-water habitat with cool-water habitats for native fish and non-native fish and crayfish. We also compare trophic positions among species.

Background and Description of Area

The Jackrabbit Spring system is located in the southeastern part of the Ash Meadows National Wildlife Refuge (AMNWR) (fig. 1.1). Its discharge in 1962 was 0.04 m³/s (Walker and Eakin, 1963). Typical for thermal springs, Jackrabbit Spring outflow cools in a downstream direction (Garside and Schilling, 1979). Water temperature in the spring-pool and discharge temperature at Jackrabbit Spring is about 26.9° C (± 1° C); water temperature 3.75 km downstream of the spring's origin can range well over 20° C (Scoppettone and others, 1995).

The Jackrabbit Spring system's biotic community has undergone substantial anthropogenic disruption. Pumping the spring system dry was the most disruptive event (Soltz and Naiman, 1978; Deacon and Williams, 1991)—both Ash Meadows pupfish (*Cyprinodon nevadensis mionectes*) and Ash Meadows speckled dace (*Rhinichthys osculus nevadensis*) were extirpated from the system (and later restocked) (Williams and Sada, 1985). Presumably, these species also entered the system from the Big Spring system to which Jackrabbit Spring was connected. Non-native sailfin molly (*Poecilia latipinna*) and western mosquitofish (*Gambusia affinis*) also reinvaded the Big Spring system. Non-native red swamp crayfish (*Procambarus*

1

clarkii) are documented to have arrived in Ash Meadows by at least the late 1930s (Miller, 1948), and may have survived the pumping events because of its ability to burrow into muddy substrate for extended periods (Hobbs and others, 1989). Bullfrogs (*Lithobates catesbeiana*) have occupied Ash Meadows spring systems since at least the late 1930s (Miller, 1948), and may have reinvaded the Jackrabbit Spring system from the Big Spring system or another proximal spring system. Red-rim malania (*Melonoides tuberculata*) probably was introduced to Ash Meadows in the early 1960s with the introduction and rearing of aquaria fish in an Ash Meadows' spring (Soltz and Naiman, 1978); when they established in the Jackrabbit Spring system is unknown, but they could have survived the pumping of the system in 1970 (Mitchell and Hobbs, 2007). Presumably, the Jackrabbit Spring system harbored a suite of thermophilic invertebrates (some of which may have been endemic), but these perished when the system dried.

Since Miller's (1948) description of pupfish in Ash Meadows, the Jackrabbit Spring outflow has been redirected from a westerly to a southerly direction. In order to improve irrigation, the channel apparently had been diverted with a small impoundment constructed about 2 km from the spring source. By the late 1990s, a segment of the spring outflow became overgrown with invasive salt cedar (*Tamarix ramosissima*), which hid the impounded stretch of stream from view. In March 2005, a fire along the Jackrabbit Spring outflow burned through the dense stand of salt cedar, exposing the impounded reaches of its outflow, and providing the opportunity to rehabilitate the channel into habitat more conducive to the native fishes (Scoppettone and others, 2005). In summer 2006, impoundments were removed and water diverted to an excavated channel; in summer 2007, property acquired by ANWR in 1996 was rehabilitated from marsh-like habitat to a well-defined channel.

Methods

Collection Site and Processing Samples

We investigated carbon flow and trophic positioning using gut content and stable isotope ($\delta^{13}C$ and $\delta^{15}N$) analysis of plant and animal tissue. Samples for this study were taken in 2009 at four sites and in four seasons along the Jackrabbit Spring system (fig. 1.1). Sites were selected to represent warm-water habitat (spring-pool and 700 m from spring-pool) and cool-water habitat (1,800 and 3,600 m from spring-pool). These selected sites were thermally characterized by placing a HOBO® onset temperature logger at each station in February 2009. HOBOs® were retrieved in October 2009; the 700-m station HOBO® was lost. Because of the importance of comparing temperature synchronously, we installed the HOBOs again in December 2009 and recovered them in October 2010.

We set five 3.3 mm mesh, standard Gee minnow traps at approximately 1 m apart to capture fishes and crayfish for stable isotope and gut analysis at each outflow station; in the spring-pool, we spaced five minnow traps equidistant within the pools. Minnow traps were baited with dog food that was wrapped in gauze to prevent food from being ingested by collected fishes and crayfish. Because sailfin molly and mosquitofish are difficult to capture with a benthically situated minnow trap, we used dip-nets proximal to the minnow traps to secure additional specimens. Captured fish were weighed and measured. Fish guts were then removed and placed in 10 percent formalin. The remainder of the fish was placed on dry ice until it could be transferred to a freezer. Up to 8 pupfish and 4 speckled dace were taken at each station, while up to 9 mosquitofish, molly, and crayfish also were collected. Benthic invertebrates were captured by stirring the stream bottom with a rebar post and capturing displaced invertebrates with a dip-net. Four samples were taken at 1-m intervals from each of the four sites. We used a 600-μm mesh plankton net to sample for free-swimming organisms in Jackrabbit Spring outflow. A 600-μm mesh plankton net was dragged across the spring-pool 10 times each season. At each station, terrestrial invertebrates were collected using dip-nets to sweep vegetation within 2 m of the outflow and stream-pool. Clips of vascular plants (aquatic and terrestrial) were taken within the same area from which terrestrial invertebrates were sampled. All items collected were labeled as to date and station, and assigned an identification number. Each sample was placed in plastic bags, put on dry ice, and transferred to a freezer.

Gut Analysis to Determine Carbon Source and Trophic Position

None of the Ash Meadows fishes and crayfish we examined has a true stomach, so we examined the anterior one-third of their guts. Gut contents were identified using a dissection microscope and placed into one of the following categories: filamentous algae; detritus; vascular plant; fish; aquatic invertebrate; terrestrial invertebrate; unidentified invertebrate; and substrate (dirt, sand, and gravel). Food items consumed were quantified by mean percent by volume (Windell, 1971). We used a Kruskal Wallis test to determine whether there was a difference in food items consumed by fish species and crayfish among stations. The Kruskal Wallis also was used to test for a propensity for fish or crayfish to prey upon aquatic invertebrates more often than terrestrial invertebrates. Because of small sample sizes, seasons were grouped together by species for analysis .

Following Vander Zanden and Rasmussen (1996), the trophic position of prey items was used to calculate the trophic position for each fish using the following formula:

$$T_a = \sum (V_i T_i) + 1,$$

where T_a = mean trophic position of the subject fish,
V_i = volumetric contribution of the ith prey item, and
T_i = trophic position of the ith food item.

Food item trophic positions were as follows: primary producers (algae, vascular plants, and detritus) were first trophic level and assigned a value of 1; aquatic invertebrates were considered to be a mixture of primary consumers (2) and secondary consumers (3), and thus given a trophic value of 2.5; and terrestrial invertebrates were a mixture of primary (2), secondary (3), and tertiary consumers (4), and assigned a trophic value of 3. Fish also were assigned a trophic value of 3.

$\delta^{13}C$ and $\delta^{15}N$ Analysis to Determine Carbon Source and Trophic Position

Stable isotopes ($\delta^{15}N$ and $\delta^{13}C$) have become a popular tool to assess trophic positioning and energy flow within an ecosystem (Peterson and Fry, 1987; Vander Zanden and Rasmussen, 1999; Post, 2002). An advantage of stable isotopes is that they give a time-integrated analysis of source of carbon input (Fry and Arnold, 1982). Primary producers typically have a distinctive $\delta^{13}C$ signature and contribute relatively minor trophic enrichment (about 0.8 percent), making their signal useful in assessing carbon source (Vander Zanden and Rasmussen, 1999). The nitrogen isotope $\delta^{15}N$ enriches 3.4 percent at each trophic level, and this magnitude is useful in calculating trophic position (Minagawa and Wada, 1984; Peterson and Fry, 1987).

We used $\delta^{13}C$ to determine if carbon source for fishes and crayfish came primarily from the stream (algae, bacteria, aquatic invertebrates) or from more of a terrestrial origin (C_3 plants, terrestrial invertebrates). Two methods were used to determine potential carbon source: (1) tracking $\delta^{13}C$ enrichment in a downstream direction, and (2) testing whether there was a significant affiliation in carbon signal among organisms. If algae are enriched in a downstream direction, it follows that organisms feeding directly or indirectly upon algae also would experience $\delta^{13}C$ enrichment. We used analysis of variance to test if there was downstream $\delta^{13}C$ enrichment for algae, C_3 plants, fishes, and crayfish between the spring-pool and the 700-m station. We restricted our analysis to the two stations from which we were successful in securing the algae $\delta^{13}C$ signal. We also used analysis of variance to test if organisms had similar $\delta^{13}C$ affiliations.

To determine trophic levels among fishes and crayfish we used the following formula from Post (2002):

$$T_{con} = T_{base} + (\delta^{15}N_{con} - \delta^{15}N_{base})/\Delta_N,$$

where T_{con} is the trophic position of the subject consumer, T_{base} is the trophic position of the organism used to estimate $\delta^{15}N_{base}$, $\delta^{15}N_{con}$ and $\delta^{15}N_{base}$ were measured directly, and Δ_N is 3.4 percent (mean enrichment per trophic level). T_{base} was 1 for primary producer and 2 for primary consumer. We used filamentous algae T_{base} 1, but only for the spring-pool and 700-m stations, because these were the only stations from which the $\delta^{15}N$ signature was available for algae. Crayfish were used for T_{base} 2 and at all stations because it was collected at all four stations in winter and summer.

For stable isotope analysis, we used our January and July collections; these two seasons represented the environmental extremes for water temperature, day length, and food availability. Samples for stable isotope analysis were sent to the UC Davis Stable Isotope Facilities. Prior to sending samples they were rinsed in deionized water, oven dried, and pulverized.

Results

Warm- and Cool-Water Habitats

The spring-pool and 700-m stations were considered warm-water habitats. Water temperatures at these two stations are fairly constant, with daily and seasonal temperature fluctuation not exceeding $3°C$, and mean daily temperature was equal to or greater than $25°C$ (fig. 1.2). For the cool-water stations (1,800-m and 3,600-m), mean daily average temperature fluctuation exceeded $4°C$ and seasonal temperature was less than $25°C$ for much of the year. Water temperature at the spring-pool, 1,800-m and 3,600-m station is shown in figure 1.2.

Seasonal Gut Analysis

In the thermal habitats (spring-pool station and 700-m station), filamentous algae was the predominant food item in the guts of Ash Meadows pupfish in all four seasons. Gut contents in the spring-pool station averaged $92.7\% \pm 14.4$ by volume (table 1.1) and a seasonal range from 82.7 to 100% (table A.1). At the 700-m station, average gut content was $86.2\% \pm 26.7$ by volume, and a seasonal range of 57.0–96.4%. Although pupfish at the two warm-water stations consumed primarily filamentous algae, the spring-pool pupfish consumed a significantly greater (df = 1, $\chi^2 = 4.393$, p = 0.036) proportion of algae than did pupfish at the 700-m station.

At the cool-water stations, the 3,600-m station algae comprised 22.2% ± 40.0 of pupfish gut contents by volume with a range of 0.0–65.2 percent among seasons (table A.1). The proportion of algae taken at the 700-m station was significantly (df = 1, χ^2 = 21.612, p = 0.001) greater than the proportion of algae taken at 3,600-m station. Only a small portion of the pupfish diet consisted of invertebrates, and most of the consumed invertebrates were aquatic (table 1.1). There was a significantly (df = 1, χ^2 = 7.010, p = 0.008) greater proportion of aquatic invertebrates taken at the 700-m station (high of 10 percent by volume taken in winter) than the spring-pool and 3,600-m stations, which only represented a high of 3.3 percent in spring-time at the spring-pool station (table 1.1). There was no significant difference (df = 2, χ^2 = 0.010, p = 0.995) in terrestrial invertebrates taken among stations. Although pupfish fed upon a very meager amount of invertebrates ($\bar{x}$ = 1.7% ± 9.0 aquatic, $\bar{x}$ = 0.7% ± 5.3 terrestrial), the volume of aquatic invertebrates was significantly greater (df = 1, χ^2 = 4.817, p = 0.028) than terrestrial invertebrates. The relative proportion of detritus consumed by pupfish increased in a downstream direction. However, there was little difference between the spring-pool station ($\bar{x}$ = 1.7%) and 700-m station ($\bar{x}$ = 2.9%); the difference was statistically significant (df = 1, χ^2 = 5.539, p = 0.019), but probably not biologically significant. Detritus was the primary food item ($\bar{x}$ = 45.3%) consumed at the 3,600-m station, and this was significantly greater (df = 1, χ^2 = 9.533, p = 0.001) than the detritus consumed at the 700-m station. There was relatively little vascular vegetation consumed by pupfish, and there was no significant difference (df = 1, χ^2 = 0.009, p = 0.924) between the spring-pool and 700-m station. There was significant difference (df = 1, χ^2 = 4.937, p = 0.026) in the relative proportion of vascular plants taken at the 700-m and 3,600-m stations. Seven of eight pupfish taken in the fall had bottom substrate (sand and pebbles) in their guts. The 1,800-m station was not included in our analysis because it was represented by only one pupfish in all four seasons.

Invertebrates were the predominant food items taken by speckled dace at three of the four stations, with aquatic invertebrates occupying a greater volume of the speckled dace's gut at three of the stations (table 1.1). However, there was no significant difference in relative amount by volume of aquatic (df = 3, χ^2 = 6.176, p = 0.103) or terrestrial invertebrates (df = 3, χ^2 = 2.572, p = 0.666) taken among stations. This was true of all other food categories; there was no difference among stations. In all four seasons and all four stations, dace took a greater proportion of aquatic invertebrates ($\bar{x}$ = 29.4%) than terrestrial invertebrates ($\bar{x}$ = 13.8%), and this difference was significant (df = 1, χ^2 = 4.442, p = 0.035).

The primary food item consumed by mosquitofish was invertebrates, with a greater volume of terrestrial invertebrates taken at each of the four stations. As with speckled dace, there was no significant difference between aquatic (df = 3, χ^2 = 5.514, p = 0.138) or terrestrial invertebrates (df = 3, χ^2 = 2.372, p = 0.499) taken among stations. Also, as with speckled dace, there was no difference in any other food category among stations. Mosquitofish did take a significantly greater (df = 1, χ^2 = 4.479, p = 0.034) percent by volume of terrestrial invertebrates ($\bar{x}$ = 27% ± 32.4) than aquatic invertebrates ($\bar{x}$ = 18.6% ± 28.4).

Sailfin molly were captured primarily in the spring-pool and 700-m stations where they fed almost exclusively upon filamentous algae and detritus. There was a significantly greater (df = 1, χ^2 = 5.375, p = 0.020) amount of algae taken by percent volume from the spring-pool, and a significantly greater (df = 1, χ^2 = 5.375, p = 0.020) amount of detritus by percent volume taken from the 700-m station.

Detritus was the predominant item consumed by crayfish at three of the four stations, but there was no significant difference (df = 3, χ^2 = 3.939, p = 0.268) in the amount taken among stations. Crayfish consumed few invertebrates, but fish and vascular plant material was found in their guts at each of the four stations. The only statistical difference (df = 1, χ^2 = 7.442, p = 0.006) in food items taken among stations was vascular plant material between the spring-pool and 700-m station.

Trophic position using gut contents indicated pupfish and sailfin molly are the primary consumers at stations in which they occur (table 1.2). Mosquitofish were second-order consumers at all stations, while speckled dace were second-order consumers in warm-water stations and were slightly more omnivorous in cool-water stations. Trophic position of crayfish indicated omnivory, but tending toward herbivory at most stations; their trophic position was slightly higher in cool-water stations.

Stable Isotopes δ^{13}C and δ^{15}N

The δ^{13}C and δ^{15}N isotopes contributed further to carbon contribution and trophic positioning as related to warm-water and cool-water habitats. We harvested algae for stable isotope in sufficient quantity in the warm-water region of the Jackrabbit Spring system (Spring-pool and 700-m stations), which appeared to be the primary carbon source for fish species captured in the thermal upper reaches of the Jackrabbit Spring system. This conclusion was derived using Kennedy's (2002) observation that there is δ^{13}C enrichment of algae in a downstream direction, and consequently the organisms depending directly and indirectly on algae as a carbon source experience δ^{13}C enrichment in a downstream direction. The enrichment from the spring-pool station to the 700-m station for algae in this study was significant (df = 1, χ^2 = 6.61, p = 0.042), but (probably due to our small sample size) did not meet the test for normality (table 1.2, fig. 1.3). There was a significant difference in C_3 plants in terms of δ^{13}C between the spring-pool and 700-m station, but this was due to δ^{13}C reduction in a downstream direction. All fishes and crayfish in our samples experienced δ^{13}C enrichment from the spring-pool to the 700-m station, and this increase was significant for all species except mosquitofish (table 1.2, fig. 1.3, 1.4). For animal species, δ^{13}C enrichment continued downstream to the 1,800-m station for all but the sailfin molly, which had very suspect δ^{13}C and δ^{15}N (discussed below). We did not use the 1,800-m station in our analysis because there were few pupfish (n = 1), and molly (n = 3) captured there.

The δ^{13}C signature was useful in assessing potential carbon connections amongst Jackrabbit Spring system organisms, including potential predator/prey and competitive interactions. Among potential fish and crayfish prey items, terrestrial invertebrates had a mean δ^{13}C -22.6 ± 3.8, compared to -28.2 ± 4.0 for aquatic invertebrates (table 1.3), and this difference was significant (table 1.4). Aquatic insects were not significantly different than algae, but terrestrial invertebrates had a significantly greater δ^{13}C signal than algae. Among fishes, pupfish had the lowest mean δ^{13}C at -27.7 (table 1.3), and this value was not significantly different from filamentous algae (-28.9) and aquatic invertebrates (-28.2) (table 1.4), suggesting that both may be a food source for pupfish. The mean δ^{13}C of C_3 plants was the same as pupfish, but the low δ^{15}N signal (3.1) from C_3 and C_4 plants all but precluded these plants as a direct carbon source of pupfish. Pupfish $\delta^{13}C$ signature was significantly different than that for terrestrial invertebrates (table 1.3). There was significant difference between the $\delta^{13}C$ signature between speckled dace and aquatic invertebrates, but not between dace and terrestrial invertebrates. Similarly, there was a significant difference between mosquitofish and aquatic invertebrates, but no difference between mosquitofish and terrestrial invertebrates.

Analysis of $\delta^{15}N$ among organisms for each of our stations in winter and summer adds more information as to items consumed over time. For example, trophic position of pupfish in January and July at the spring-pool ranged from 2.4 to 2.6 using algae as the producer base, and 2.5 using crayfish as the primary consumer base suggesting pupfish are more omnivorous than portrayed by gut analysis (table 1.5). Speckled dace held the highest trophic position for each station for each season. Mosquitofish had a trophic position similar to pupfish at most stations in January and July (table 1.5). Crayfish were always lowest in $\delta^{15}N$ and, hence, lowest in trophic order relative to fishes.

Pupfish, speckled dace, and mosquitofish generally had higher trophic position in winter than summer, suggesting invertebrates were a more important food source in winter. Trophic position for pupfish (3.0 using algae base and crayfish base) in January at the upper station was exceedingly high for a species for which filamentous algae is a primary contributor to the diet. The value of sailfin molly (2.7), which is primarily herbivorous, also is unexpectedly high.

Discussion

Gut analysis indicated that filamentous algae were the predominant food item consumed by pupfish in warm water for all four seasons. The warm, open water of the upper reaches of the Jackrabbit Spring system was particularly favorable to pupfish because it promotes year-round growth of filamentous algae (Kennedy and Hobbie, 2004; Kennedy and others, 2006). The $\delta^{13}C$ signature of Ash Meadows pupfish also suggested an algal affiliation, as did the enrichment of $\delta^{13}C$ in both algae and Ash Meadows pupfish in warm-water habitat.

Although filamentous algae appears to be important food stuff (Naiman, 1975; Kennedy and others, 2006), there are questions about its digestibility (Naiman, 1979). Microbial organisms associated with filamentous algae may be sufficiently small to be rapidly digested and hence not readily detected in gut analysis; however, they may contribute to pupfish diet and enhance the $\delta^{15}N$ signal. Analysis of pupfish trophic position using $\delta^{15}N$ indicated primary consumers contribute substantially to their nutriment, especially in winter, and more so than inferred from our gut analysis. Our trophic positioning for Ash Meadows pupfish was slightly higher than that observed by Kennedy and others (2006). Plausible explanations are habitat changes (fire and restoration) and the substantial temporal and spatial variation in $\delta^{13}C$ and $\delta^{15}N$ within an aquatic system (Boon and Bunn, 1994; Vander Zanden and others, 1997).

Among Ash Meadow fishes, pupfish exhibited the most dramatic change in gut contents between the warm- and cool-water stations. At the 3,600-m station, pupfish consumed detritus, algae, and substrate. Substrate (sand, gravel) was found in the guts of all eight pupfish collected in the fall (November). Whether substrate is associated with acquiring some food stuff from the stream bottom is unknown, but substrate also has been taken in substantial amounts from the guts of Devils Hole pupfish (*Cyprinodon diabolis*) (Minckley and Deacon, 1975; Wilson and Blinn, 2007) and desert pupfish (*Cyprinodon macularius*) (Naiman, 1979).

Speckled dace also are bottom oriented, but in the spring-brooks of Ash Meadows, they feed primarily on drift, working the entire water column (Scoppettone and others, 1995); stable isotope analysis indicates they rely primarily upon terrestrial invertebrates. Perhaps a reason for reliance on terrestrial invertebrates is that the Jackrabbit Spring system harbored few native aquatic invertebrates, especially in its upper reaches (Andrews and others, unpub. data, 2006). Mosquitofish generally are surface oriented and have a body form adapted to taking prey from the water surface–the head is flattened and mouth dorsally situated (Swanson and others, 1996), thus they are perfectly suited for preying upon terrestrial insects that fall or land on the water surface. Speckled dace $\delta^{13}C$ value was not significantly different from that of terrestrial insects. It was therefore surprising that dace had a mean $\delta^{15}N$ value identical to pupfish for all four stations and two seasons, and that they had close or identical trophic positions at co-occurring stations. Mosquitofish are opportunistic omnivores and may feed on algae and plants, along with terrestrial and aquatic invertebrates (Harrington and Harrington, 1961), and this may account, in part, for the similar $\delta^{15}N$. However, a more plausible explanation is that the $\delta^{15}N$ we experienced in the Jackrabbit Spring system was fairly high (5.7), and close to the magnitude of terrestrial and aquatic invertebrates (6.6). Speckled dace held the highest trophic position at each station, indicating that this species secured more invertebrates than did mosquitofish.

Sailfin molly tend toward herbivory (Meffe and Snelson, 1989), and our stable isotope analysis put them at the lowest trophic position among the fishes. From our data, we were unable to determine if the lower $\delta^{15}N$ signal is the result of molly consuming greater amounts of vascular plant materials. Gut analysis indicated that molly compete with pupfish for algae and detritus. Western mosquitofish have been described as opportunistic omnivores, feeding on a broad array of food items (Swanson and others, 1996). In this study, gut analysis suggested that mosquitofish, along with speckled dace, held the highest trophic position among fishes and crayfish, but $\delta^{15}N$ analysis put mosquitofish into a lower trophic position similar to pupfish. Because stable isotopes offer a time-integrated perspective of diet (Fry and Arnold, 1982), we concluded that in the newly restored Jackrabbit Spring system, mosquitofish were more herbivorous than speckled dace through much of the year. Our results differ from Kennedy and others (2006), who attributed a higher trophic position than this study. Western mosquitofish are specialized feeders, and the invertebrates they consume typically are terrestrial types (Moyle, 2002) that probably were more available during the Kennedy and others (2006) study. Their study was pre-restoration, and focused on a densely covered reach of stream where terrestrial invertebrates were in much greater availability than the sparser riparian corridor present at the time of our study.

Crayfish are known for their catholic diet, consuming vascular plant detritus, algae, and animal matter, thus exploiting all carbon sources in a system (Whitledge and Rabeni, 1997; Kennedy and others, 2006). Because of their dietary diversity, crayfish exert a major influence on the flow of energy; they are often predominant in bio-mass and compete with native and non-native fishes (Momot, 1995). Although we did not compare relative bio-mass in this study, we observed that red swamp crayfish bio-mass far exceeds that of native fishes. Although crayfish consumed primarily vegetative material, they are sufficiently numerous that they may consume substantial amounts of aquatic invertebrates, fish eggs, and larvae. Judging from results of stable isotope analysis, crayfish benefited most from C_3 vascular plant input, and this is consistent with other studies indicating vascular plants to be a substantial contribution to the crayfish diet (Kennedy and others, 2006). We suspect the crayfish population may grow with additional vascular plant contribution, including allochthonous materials.

Native fish diets observed in this study may be different than what occurred prior to manipulation of the Ash Meadows ecosystem. Anthropogenic changes to the landscape (including shifts in vegetation composition, extinction and extirpation of native aquatic organisms, and introduction of non-native aquatic species) have altered flow of energy in Ash Meadows Spring systems, including flow of energy to native fishes. Non-native species can cause a shift in diet and habitat use of native species, and without such a shift natives may face competitive exclusion. Our study suggests that, under current conditions, filamentous algae is important to the diet of Ash Meadows pupfish, and habitat conditions that foster algae growth should be considered in the rehabilitation and long-term management of spring systems. For speckled dace, invertebrate production and their availability for consumption should be target considerations in habitat rehabilitation.

Acknowledgments

We thank Ash Meadows National Wildlife Refuge for funding this study. Bryan Hobbs (U.S. Fish and Wildlife Service) assisted with fish collections. We also thank Tom Strekal and Mark Fabes (U.S. Geological Survey) for reviewing the manuscript.

References Cited

Andrews, K., Scoppettone, G.G., and Johnson, D., 2006, Survey of invertebrates in Jackrabbit Spring after a fire: U.S.G.S Biological Resources Discipline, Reno Field Station, unpublished report, 5 p.

Boon, P.I., and Bunn, S.E., 1994, Variations in the stable isotope composition of aquatic plants and their implications for food web analysis: Aquatic Botany, v. 48, p. 99–108.

Deacon, J.E., and Williams, C.D., 1991, Ash Meadows and the legacy of the Devils Hole pupfish, *in* Minckley, W.L., and Deacon, J.E., eds., Battle against extinction— native fish management in the American West: Tucson, The University of Arizona Press, p. 69–87.

Fry, B., and Arnold, C., 1982, Rapid C-13/C-12 turnover during growth of brown shrimp (Penaeus-*Aztecus*): Oecologia, v. 54, p. 200–204.

Garside, L.I., and Schilling, J.H., 1979, Thermal waters of Nevada: Reno, University of Nevada, Nevada Bureau of Mines and Geology, Mackay School of Mines, Bulletin 91.

Harrington, R.W., Jr., and Harrington, E.S., 1961, Food selection among fishes invading a high subtropical salt marsh—from onset of flooding through the progress of a mosquito brood: Ecology, v. 42, p. 646–665.

Hobbs, H.H., III, Jass, J.P., and Huner, J.V., 1989, A review of global crayfish introductions with particular emphasis on two North American species (Decapoda, Cambaridae): Crustaceana, v. 56, p. 300–316.

Kennedy, T.A., 2002, The causes and consequences of plant invasions: St. Paul, Minnesota, University of Minnesota, Ph.D. dissertation, 145 p.

Kennedy, T.A., Finlay, J.C., and Hobbie, S.E., 2006, Eradication of invasive *Tamarix ramosissima* along a desert stream increases native fish density: Ecological Application, v. 15, p. 2,072–2,083.

Kennedy, T.A., and Hobbie, S.E., 2004, Saltcedar (*Tamarix ramosissima*) invasion alters organic matter dynamics in a desert stream: Freshwater Biology, v. 49, p. 65–76.

Meffe, G.K., and Snelson, F.F., Jr., 1989, Ecology and evolution of livebearing fishes (Poeciliidae): Englewood Cliffs, N.J., Prentice-Hall, p. 18–21.

Miller, R.R., 1948, The cyprinodont fishes of Death Valley system of eastern California and southeastern Nevada: Miscellaneous Publications of the Museum of Zoology, v. 529, 55 p.

Minagawa, M., and Wada, E., 1984, Stepwise enrichment of ^{15}N along food chains—further evidence and relation between ^{15}N and animal age: Geochimica et Cosmochimica Acta, v. 48, p. 1,135–1,140.

Minckley, C.O., and Deacon, J.E., 1975, Foods of Devils Hole pupfish *Cyprinodon diabolis* (Cyprinidae): Southwestern Naturalist, v. 20, p. 105–111.

Mitchell, A.J., and Hobbs, M.S., 2007, The effect of chemical treatments on red-rim melania *Melanoides tuberculata*, an exotic aquatic snail that serves as a vector of trematodes to fish and other species in the USA: North American Journal of Fisheries Management, v. 27, p. 1,287–1,293.

Momot, W.T., 1995, Redefining the role of crayfish in aquatic ecosystems: Reviews in Fisheries Science, v. 3, p. 33–63.

Moyle, P.B., 2002, Inland fishes of California, revised and expanded: Berkeley, California, University of California Press, 517 p.

Naiman, R.J., 1975, Food habits of the Amargosa pupfish in a thermal stream: Transactions of the American Fisheries Society, v. 104, p. 536–538.

Naiman, R.J., 1979, Preliminary food studies of *Cyprinodon macularias* and *Cyprinidon nevadensis* (Cyprinodontidae): The Southwestern Naturalist, v. 24, p. 538–541.

Peterson, B.J., and Fry, B., 1987, Stable isotopes in ecosystem studies: Annual Review of Ecology and Systematics, v. 18, p. 293–320.

Post, D.M., 2002, Using stable isotopes to estimate trophic position—Models, methods and assumptions: Ecology, v. 83, p. 703–718.

Scoppettone, G.G., Rissler, P.H., Gourley, C., and Martinez, C., 2005, Habitat restoration as a means of controlling non-native fish in a Mojave Desert Oasis: Restoration Ecology, v. 13, p. 247–256.

Scoppettone, G.G., Rissler, P.H., Byers, S., Shea, S., Nielsen, B., and Sjöberg, J., 1995, Information on the status and ecology of Ash Meadows Fishes and *Ambrysus*: National Biological Service, Reno Field Station, 111 p.

Soltz, K.L. and Naiman, R.J., 1978, The natural history of native fishes in the Death Valley system: Natural History Museum of Los Angeles County, California: Science Series, v. 30, 76 p.

Swanson, C., Cech Jr., J., and Piedrahita, R.H., 1996, Mosquitofish-biology, culture and use in mosquito control: Mosquito and Vector Control Association of California and The University of California Mosquito Research Program, 88 p.

Vander Zanden, M.J. and Rasmussen, J.B., 1996, A trophic position model of pelagic food webs—Impact on contaminant biomagnifications in lake trout: Ecological Monograph, v. 66, p. 451–477.

Vander Zanden, M.J., Cabana, G., and Rasmussen, J.B., 1997, Comparing trophic position of freshwater fish calculated using stable nitrogen isotopes ratios (δ^{15}N) and literature dietary data: Canadian Journal of Aquatic Sciences, v. 54, p. 1,142–1,158.

Vander Zanden, M.J., and Rasmussen, J.B., 1999, Primary consumer δ^{13}C and δ^{15}N and the trophic position of aquatic consumers: Ecology, v. 80, p. 1,395-1,405.

Walker, G.E., and Eakin, T.E., 1963, Geology and ground water of Amargosa Desert, Nevada-California: Ground-Water Resources-Reconnaissance Series, Report 14.

Whitledge, G.W., and Rabeni, C.F., 1997, Energy Sources and ecological role of crayfishes in an Ozark stream—Insights from stable isotopes and gut analysis: Canadian Journal of Aquatic Sciences, v. 54, p. 2,555-2,563.

Williams, J.E., and Sada, D.W., 1985, Status of two endangered fishes, *Cyrpinodon nevadensis mionectes* and *Rhinichthys osculus nevadensis*, from two springs in Ash Meadows, Nevada: Southwestern Naturalist, v. 30, p. 475–484.

Wilson, K.P., and Blinn, D.W., 2007, Food Web structure energetic, and importance of allochthonous carbon in a desert cavernous limnocrene: Devils Hole, Nevada, v. 67, p. 185–198.

Windell, J.J., 1971, Food analysis and rate of digestion, *in* Ricker W.E., ed., Methods for assessment of production in fresh water: Oxford and Edinburgh, U.K., Blackwell Scientific Publications, IBP Handbook 3, p. 215–226.

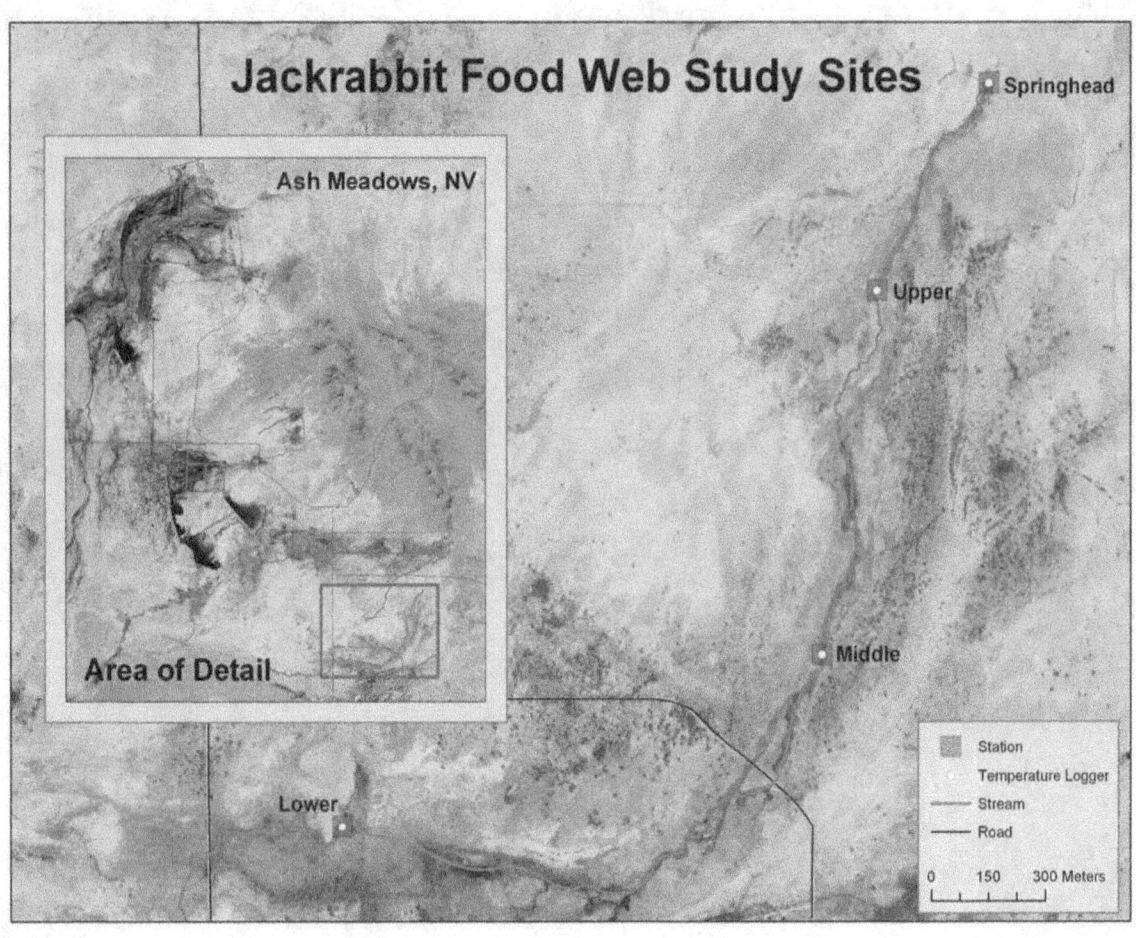

Figure 1.1. Location of four stations for carbon source and trophic position of Ash Meadows fishes and crayfish. (Inset) Jackrabbit Spring system in relationship to Ash Meadows National Wildlife Refuge.

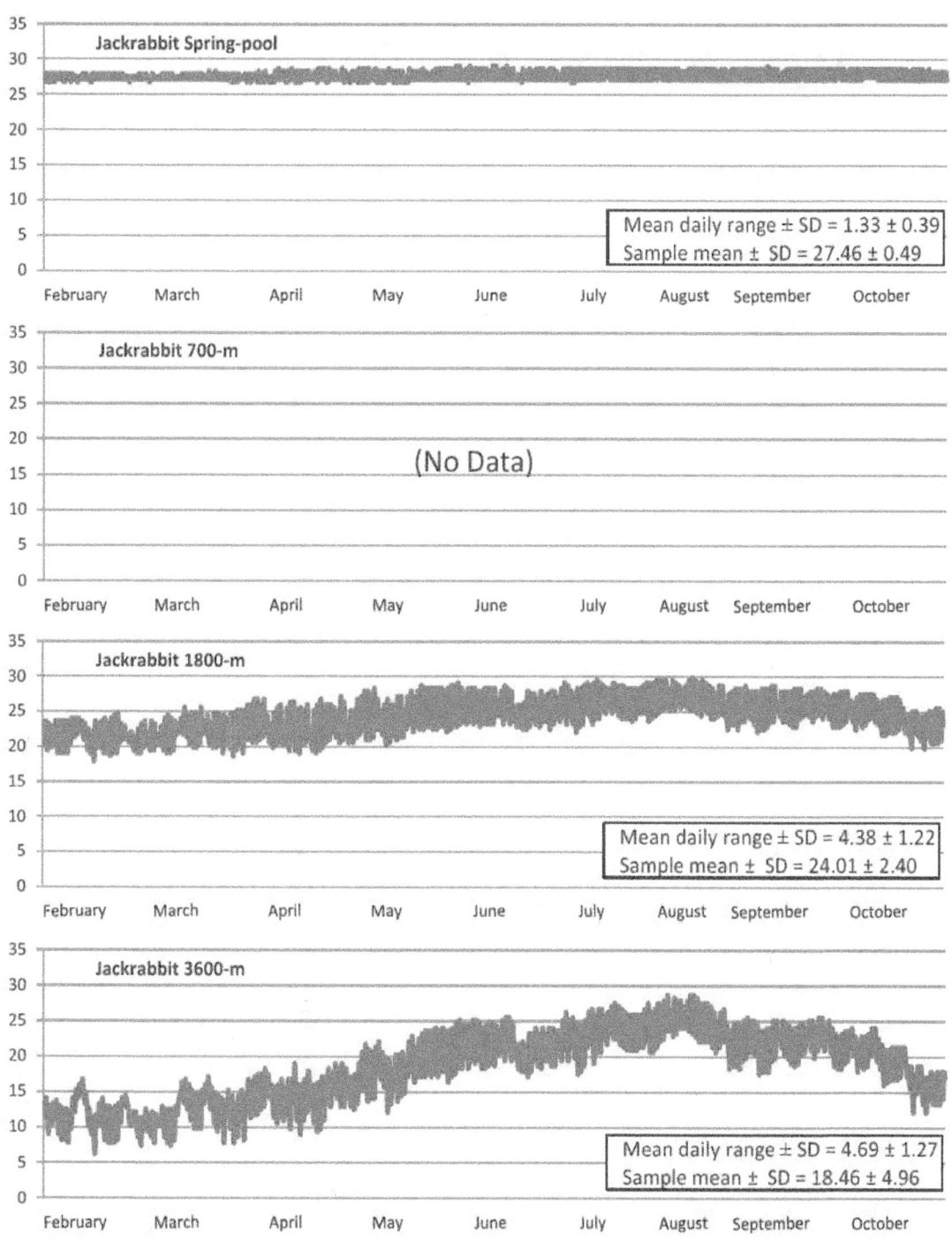

Figure 1.2. Water temperatures taken from December 2009 through October 2010 at four stations along Jackrabbit Spring system.

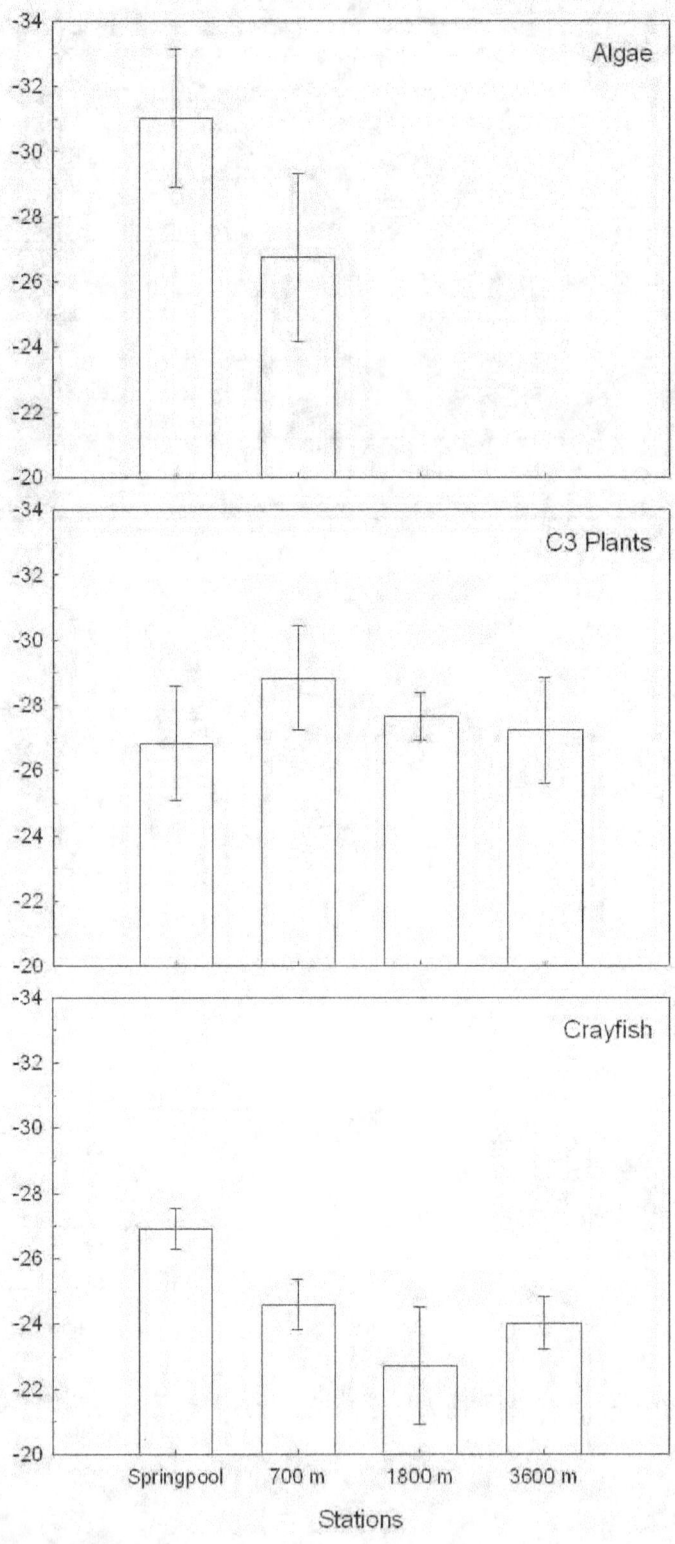

Figure 1.3. Relative δ¹³C in algae, C₃ plants, and crayfish at four stations along the Jackrabbit Spring system.

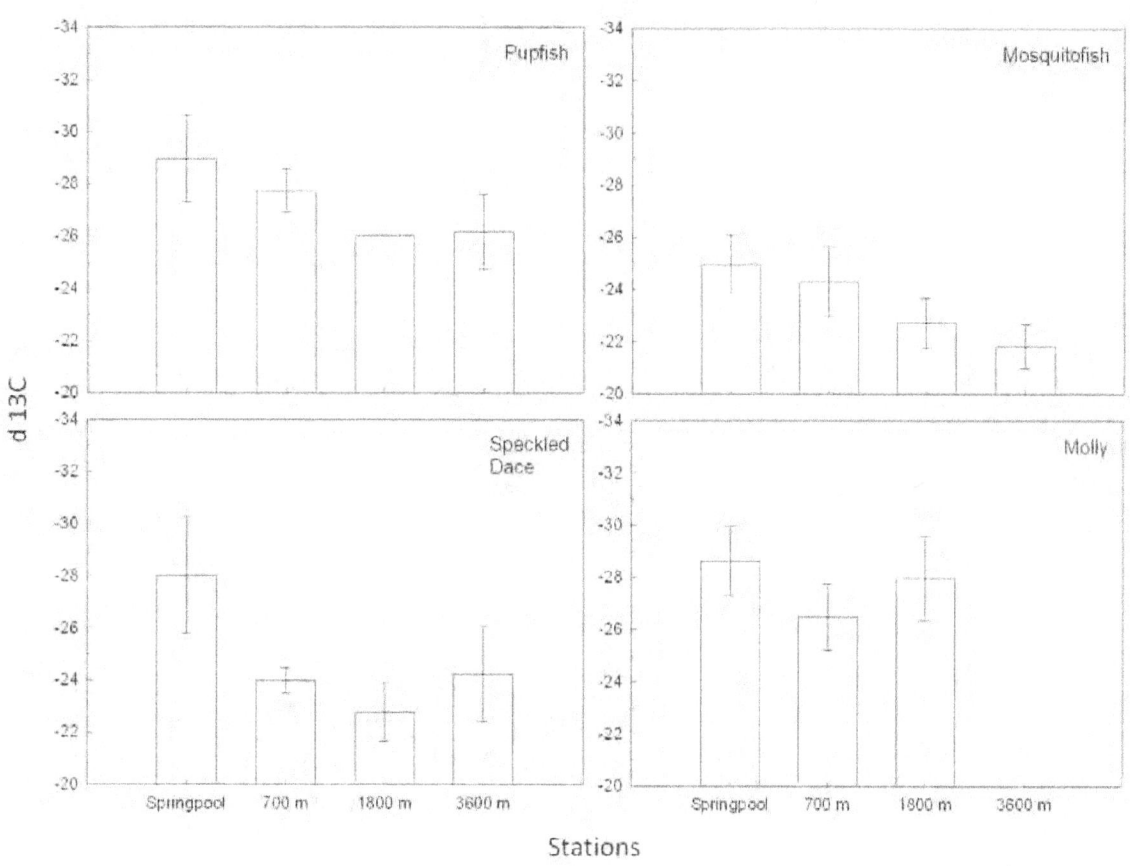

Figure 1.4. Relative δ¹³C in four Ash Meadows fishes at four stations along the Jackrabbit Spring system.

Table 1.1. Gut content, mean percent by volume, and standard deviation of Ash Meadows fishes and crayfish for all seasons at four stations.

[Number of fish or crayfish with empty guts is shown in parentheses ()]

	pupfish			
	Spring-Pool	700-m	1800-m	3600-m
Algae	92.7 ± 14.4	86.2 ± 26.7	-	22.2 ± 40.0
Vegetation	0.2 ± 0.9	0.8 ± 0.9	-	4.7 ± 11.7
Detritus	1.6 ± 6.3	2.9 ± 4.4	-	45.3 ± 46.5
Substrate	3.7 ± 10.9	5.1 ± 20.1	-	25.7 ± 43.6
Fish	0.6 ± 3.5	1.1 ± 4.1	-	0.1 ± 0.4
Aquatic Invertebrate	0.8 ± 4.6	4.4 ± 15.3	-	0.2 ± 1.0
Terrestial Invertebrate	0.2 ± 0.9	0.2 ± 0.9	-	1.7 ± 9.1
Unknown Invertebrate	0.3 ± 1.8	0.0 ± 0.0	-	0.0 ± 0.0
	N = 32 (0)	N = 28 (0)		N = 30 (0)

	speckled dace			
	Spring-Pool	700-m	1800-m	3600-m
Algae	10.7 ± 28.3	21.8 ± 35.4	16.2 ± 35.5	2.5 ± 9.2
Vegetation	1.9 ± 4.9	1.0 ± 3.2	0.0 ± 0.0	0.0 ± 0.0
Detritus	14.3 ± 37.8	25.2 ± 46.6	59.0 ± 37.5	37.9 ± 45.9
Substrate	1.4 ± 3.8	0.0 ± 0.0	0.0 ± 0.0	0.0 ± 0.0
Fish	1.7 ± 4.5	1.0 ± 3.2	0.2 ± 0.8	7.7 ± 27.7
Aquatic Invertebrate	45.0 ± 49.2	13.3 ± 31.4	12.7 ± 29.8	49.4 ± 47.5
Terrestial Invertebrate	25.0 ± 43.3	27.1 ± 44.3	8.8 ± 19.2	2.5 ± 8.9
Unknown Invertebrate	0.0 ± 0.0	10.6 ± 31.5	3.2 ± 11.4	0.0 ± 0.0
	N = 7 (5)	N = 10 (3)	N = 13 (0)	N = 13 (0)

	mosquitofish			
	Spring-Pool	700-m	1800-m	3600-m
Algae	17.5 ± 37.3	13.0 ± 24.4	3.4 ± 11.7	4.2 ± 20.4
Vegetation	0.0 ± 0.0	0.3 ± 1.8	5.7 ± 18.8	6.3 ± 17.0
Detritus	16.1 ± 28.1	33.1 ± 40.2	43.1 ± 42.3	27.8 ± 32.0
Substrate	0.0 ± 0.0	0.2 ± 0.9	0.0 ± 0.0	3.6 ± 17.8
Fish	2.3 ± 9.0	0.9 ± 4.9	0.0 ± 0.0	0.3 ± 1.4
Aquatic Invertebrate	23.1 ± 32.9	18.7 ± 28.4	11.0 ± 24.4	21.0 ± 28.4
Terrestial Invertebrate	37.0 ± 36.1	22.2 ± 29.6	26.1 ± 35.9	26.3 ± 29.6
Unknown Invertebrate	4.1 ± 15.2	11.5 ± 27.1	10.7 ± 21.3	10.6 ± 18.2
	N = 20 (8)	N = 30 (0)	N = 22 (0)	N = 24 (2)

Table 1.1. Gut content, mean percent by volume, and standard deviation of Ash Meadows fishes and crayfish for all seasons at four stations.—Continued

[Number of fish or crayfish with empty guts is shown in parentheses ()]

	sailfin molly			
	Spring-Pool	700-m	1800-m	3600-m
Algae	84.1 ± 34.7	15.0 ± 24.0	-	-
Vegetation	0.4 ± 2.1	0.0 ± 0.0	-	-
Detritus	14.3 ± 34.5	54.5 ± 52.2	-	-
Substrate	1.1 ± 5.2	30.5 ± 38.8	-	-
Fish	0.0 ± 0.0	0.0 ± 0.0	-	-
Aquatic Invertebrate	0.0 ± 0.0	0.0 ± 0.0	-	-
Terrestial Invertebrate	0.0 ± 0.0	0.0 ± 0.0	-	-
Unknown Invertebrate	0.0 ± 0.0	0.0 ± 0.0	-	-
	N = 23 (1)	N = 11 (0)		

	crayfish			
	Spring-Pool	700-m	1800-m	3600-m
Algae	15.6 ± 32.3	11.1 ± 30.3	25.2 ± 42.1	0.0 ± 0.0
Vegetation	19.5 ± 26.7	4.1 ± 13.7	5.6 ± 16.7	30.0 ± 33.2
Detritus	55.0 ± 40.7	65.8 ± 43.5	47.4 ± 45.9	35.7 ± 47.6
Substrate	0.5 ± 0.2	4.3 ± 9.5	0.0 ± 0.0	14.1 ± 29.9
Fish	9.0 ± 21.1	7.0 ± 21.8	10.0 ± 30.0	20.0 ± 38.3
Aquatic Invertebrate	0.9 ± 3.4	0.2 ± 1.0	0.7 ± 1.7	0.1 ± 0.4
Terrestial Invertebrate	0.1 ± 0.4	4.3 ± 20.9	0.0 ± 0.0	0.0 ± 0.0
Unknown Invertebrate	0.0 ± 0.0	3.0 ± 14.6	11.1 ± 33.3	0.0 ± 0.0
	N = 20 (1)	N = 23 (4)	N = 9 (8)	N = 7 (15)

Table1.2. Analysis of variance of difference in $\delta^{13}C$ between spring-pool and 700-m in algae, C_3 plants, fishes, and crayfish.

	df	F-ratio	P-value
Plants			
Algae	1(6)	6.610	0.042
C_3	1(14)	5.607	*0.033
Fishes			
pupfish	1(30)	6.939	0.013
dace	1(9)	19.081	0.002
mosquitofish	1(27)	2.240	0.146
sailfin molly	1(13)	9.043	0.010
Invertebrates			
crayfish	1(28)	81.267	0.000

* Significant reduction in $\delta^{13}C$ from Spring-pool station to 700-m station.

Table 1.3. Descriptive statistics for ^{13}C in algae, aquatic invertebrates, terrestial invertebrates, fishes, and crayfish of all four stations and two seasons in the Jackrabbit Spring system.

Organism	^{13}C	SD	^{15}N	SD
Algae	-28.9	3.2	5.7	1.3
Aquatic Invertebrates	-28.2	4.0	6.6	1.9
Terrestial Invertebrates	-22.6	3.8	6.6	2.7
pupfish	-27.7	1.7	10.2	1.3
speckled dace	-24.6	2.4	11.2	1.3
mosquitofish	-23.4	1.6	10.2	1.6
sailfin molly	-27.9	1.6	9.8	0.6
crayfish	-24.8	1.7	8.0	1.1
C_3 plants	-27.7	1.6	3.1	2.8
C_4 plants	-14.2	0.7	2.1	3.3

Table 1.4. Mann-Whitney V test to determine if there is a significant difference in $\delta^{13}C$ signal between potential prey items and potential prey item, and between fishes and crayfish and potential prey.

<u>Potential Prey Items</u>

Organisms	df	χ^2	P
Aquatic vs. Terrestial Invertebrates	1	11.84	0.001
Algae vs. Aquatic Invertebrates	1	*0.02	0.887
Algae vs. Terrestial Invertebrates	1	12.40	0.000

<u>Fishes and Crayfish and Potential Food Items</u>

	df	χ^2	P
pupfish vs. Aquatic Invertebrates	1	*0.92	0.337
speckled dace vs. Aquatic Invertebrates	1	9.35	0.002
mosquitofish vs. Aquatic Invertebrates	1	16.37	0.000
pupfish vs. Terrestrial Invertebrates	1	34.46	0.000
speckled dace vs. Terrestrial Invertebrates	1	*1.77	0.184
mosquitofish vs. Terrestial Invertebrates	1	*0.07	0.788
pupfish vs. Algae	1	*2.64	0.105
speckled dace vs. Algae	1	9.15	0.002
mosquitofish vs. Algae	1	15.43	0.000
sailfin molly vs. Algae	1	*0.44	0.505
crayfish vs. Algae	1	11.93	0.001

* Denotes no significant difference

Table 1.5. Calculated trophic position for four stations along the Jackrabbit Spring system.

Warm-Water Stations

Spring-pool

Species	δ^{15}N January	δ^{15}N July	Producer base January	Producer base July	Primary consumer base January	Primary consumer base July
pupfish	10.52	10.89	2.6	2.4	2.5	2.5
speckled dace	12.06	12.14	3.1	2.8	3.0	2.9
mosquitofish	10.36	10.36	2.6	2.2	2.5	2.4
sailfin molly	8.83	9.84	2.1	2.1	2.0	2.2
crayfish	8.79	9.14	2.1	1.9	2.0	2.0

700-m

Species	δ^{15}N January	δ^{15}N July	Producer base January	Producer base July	Primary consumer base January	Primary consumer base July
pupfish	11.15	11.13	3.0	2.4	3.0	2.7
speckled dace	12.09	11.93	3.3	2.5	3.3	3.0
mosquitofish	11.16	11.76	3.0	2.5	3.0	2.9
sailfin molly	10.11	10.00	2.7	2.0	2.7	2.4
crayfish	7.82	8.64	2.0	1.6	2.0	2.0

Cool-Water Stations

1800-m

Species	δ^{15}N January	δ^{15}N July	Producer base January	Producer base July	Primary consumer base January	Primary consumer base July
pupfish	-	-	-	-	-	-
speckled dace	11.27	11.28	-	-	3.0	2.8
mosquitofish	10.91	10.55	-	-	2.9	2.6
sailfin molly	-	10.46	-	-	-	-
crayfish	7.74	8.45	-	-	2.0	2.0

3600-m

Species	δ^{15}N January	δ^{15}N July	Producer base January	Producer base July	Primary consumer base January	Primary consumer base July
pupfish	9.04	8.00	-	-	2.7	2.0
speckled dace	9.66	9.41	-	-	2.9	2.6
mosquitofish	8.71	9.22	-	-	2.6	2.6
sailfin molly	-	-	-	-	-	-
crayfish	6.65	7.32	-	-	2.0	2.0

Relative Abundance and Distribution of Ash Meadows Pupfish and Ash Meadows Speckled Dace in the Upper One-Third of the Jackrabbit Spring System: Post-Fire and Restoration

By G. Gary Scoppettone, Mark Hereford, and Danielle Johnson, U.S. Geological Survey

Ash Meadows National Wildlife Refuge (AMNWR) in southern Nevada was established in 1984 to protect and perpetuate the highest occurrence of endemic species within the continental United States (Sada, 1990; Deacon and Williams, 1991). A particular area of concern was the protection of the Ash Meadows Native Fish assemblage that had been reduced in number due to habitat alteration and the introduction of non-native species. To improve the status of these fishes, AMNWR personnel have actively been restoring spring systems, including spring-pools and outflows; they also have eliminated non-native species from several spring systems (St. George, 1999; Weissenfluh, 2008, 2011).

Restoration of the Jackrabbit Spring system was important because it was the stronghold for the Ash Meadows speckled dace (*Rhinichthys osculus nevadensis*) and supported a sizeable population of Ash Meadows pupfish (*Cyprinodon nevadensis mionectes*) (Scoppettone and others, 2011). Ash Meadows pupfish density declined in the Jackrabbit Spring outflow in the early 1990s (Scoppettone and others, 1995). Within that time period, the reaches of the outflow channel became increasingly clogged with *Phragmites* and *Scirpus*, and there was increased canopy formation in other reaches created by *Tamarix* and *Phragmites*. Reduction of sunlight, especially caused by *Tamarix*, has been demonstrated to reduce Ash Meadows' native fish populations (Kennedy and others, 2006). Another vegetative change to the Jackrabbit Spring systems occurred in March 2005 when a fire swept through the upper reach and denuded the streambanks. The fire presented the opportunity to rehabilitate the stream outflow, and create habitat favoring native fishes over invasive species (Scoppettone and others, 2005).

The purpose of this survey was to document native fish distribution and relative abundance in a rehabilitated spring system as baseline information for evaluating future changes.

Methods

We used masks and snorkels to count speckled dace and pupfish in the upper 2.25 km of the Jackrabbit Spring system, which included the restoration area. Counts were conducted in spring 2007 and spring 2010, and were compared to a count made in spring 2006 (post-fire and pre-stream rehabilitation). Snorkel counts began 2.25 km from the spring-head, with the snorkeler crawling upstream. When pupfish or speckled dace were sighted, the number was vocalized to a data recorder who used a Garmin[TM] GPS to mark the location of each sighting.

Results

In 2006, only 378 pupfish were counted along the study reach, compared to 655 in 2007 and 1,066 in 2010 (figs. 2.1, 2.2, and 2.3). In 2006, more than 95 percent of the pupfish counted were in the spring-pool and upstream of the rehabilitation site (fig. 2.1). By spring 2010, almost 25 percent of the pupfish counted were within the rehabilitation reach. In 2006, more than 1,067 pupfish were counted even though dense vegetation kept us from snorkeling the entire 2.25 km reach. Most dace (n = 511) were sighted in the upper 800 m, and immediately upstream of the reach of stream to be rehabilitated (fig. 2.4). In 2007, there was a slight decrease in total number of dace (n = 971), and the greatest number (n = 440) was along the rehabilitated reach (fig. 2.5). However, by 2010 only 437 dace were counted, but more than 40 percent of these were along the rehabilitation site (fig. 2.6).

Discussion

The March 2005 fire and subsequent rehabilitation of the Jackrabbit outflow appears to have had a positive effect on the Ash Meadows pupfish population, presumably by increasing foraging and reproductive opportunities and reducing invasive fishes and crayfish. The fire's elimination of a localized, dense canopy of salt cedar not only facilitated stream rehabilitation but also exposed the system to increased sunlight, which presumably stimulated algal growth. Filamentous algae is the Amargosa pupfish's primary food item (Naiman, 1975; Soltz and Naiman, 1978; Moyle, 2002).

There was a substantial shift in the abundance and distribution of native fish pre- and post- rehabilitation of Jackrabbit Spring. Ash Meadows pupfish increased in number from 2006 to 2010, while speckled dace numbers decreased. Habitat rehabilitation is suspected to have expanded pupfish reproductive habitat. Jackrabbit Spring is a fairly cool thermal spring with spring-pool temperature about 26.4° C. Minimum water temperature for Amargosa pupfish reproduction is between 25 and 26° C (Soltz and Naiman, 1978), and thermal springs generally cool as they flow downstream (Garside and Schilling, 1979). Reverting marsh-like habitat to a flowing stream sustained the minimum water temperature required for reproduction farther downstream; it also served to reduce habitat for sailfin molly, mosquitofish, and crayfish (Scoppettone and others, 2005). Our food-habitat analysis indicated that sailfin molly compete for algae, and because they have been documented to be cannibalistic (Meffe and Snelson, 1989), they also may prey on larvae of other fishes, as found for shortfin molly (*Pecilia Mexicana*) (Scoppettone, 1993). Mosquitofish are voracious predators of fish larvae (Meffe, 1985), and diet analysis indicated there is resource competition, especially with speckled dace.

Speckled dace numbers were highest in 2006 when pupfish numbers were near their lowest, and were lowest in 2010 when pupfish numbers were highest. As a result of outflow manipulation, the stream maintains a warmer water temperature over a longer stream reach, which may lead to male pupfish dispersing over a wider range. Male pupfish establish reproductive territories, and aggressively chase other fishes from their respective territory including speckled dace (Lema and Nevitt, 2004). An alternate hypothesis as to why speckled dace numbers were highest several months post-fire is that they were the most successful species to pioneer the habitat after a major perturbation. Presumably, the fire reduced the number of crayfish, mosquitofish, and molly, thus improving habitat conditions for speckled dace, which are quite mobile and fairly abundant downstream of the stream reach impacted by the fire.

The snorkel surveys of Jackrabbit Spring outflow were conducted before and after a period of system disturbance, fire followed by outflow manipulation. These perturbations influence fish community structure (Moyle and Baltz, 1985); thus, the relative abundance and distribution when the stream reaches climax condition may be substantially different from what we observed in our surveys. Perhaps the most influential component to aquatic community structure is the vegetative climax, which may have a profound effect on native fish distribution and abundance (Kennedy and others, 2006; Scoppettone and others, 2011).

22

Acknowledgments

We thank the Ash Meadows National Wildlife Refuge for funding this study. We thank Tom Strekal (Bureau of Indian Affairs, retired) and Mark Fabes (U.S. Geological Survey) for their critical review.

References Cited

Deacon, J.E., and Williams, C.D., 1991, Ash Meadows and the legacy of the Devils Hole pupfish, *in* Minckley, W.L., and Deacon, J.E., eds,. Battle against extinction—Native fish management in the American West: Tucson, The University of Arizona Press, p. 69–87.

Garside, L.I., and Schilling, J.H., 1979, Thermal Waters of Nevada: Reno, University of Nevada, Nevada Bureau of Mines and Geology, Mackay School of Mines, Bulletin 91.

Kennedy, T.A., Finlay, J.C., and Hobbie, S.E., 2006, Eradication on invasive *Tamarix ramosissima* along a desert stream increases native fish density: Ecological Application, v. 15, p. 2,072–2,083.

Lema, S.C., and Nevitt, G.A., 2004, Exogenous vasotocin alters aggression during agonistic exchanges in male Amargosa River pupfish (*Cyprinodon nevadensis amargosae*): Hormones and Behavior, v. 46, p. 628–637.

Meffe, G.K., 1985, Predation and species replacement in American southwestern states—A case study: Southwestern Naturalist, v. 30, p. 173–187.

Meffe, G.K., and Snelson, F.F., Jr., 1989, An Ecological Overview of Poeciliid Fishes, *in* Meffe, G.K., and Snelson, F.F., Jr., eds., Ecology and evolution of livebearing fishes (Poeciliidae): Englewood Cliffs, New Jersey, Prentice Hall, p. 13–31.

Moyle, P.B., 2002, Inland fishes of California, revised and expanded: Berkeley, California, University of California Press, 517 p.

Moyle, P.B., and Baltz, D.M., 1985, Microhabitat use by an assemblage of California stream fishes; Developing criteria for instream flow determination: Transactions of the American Fisheries Society, v. 114, p. 695–704.

Naiman, R.J., 1975, Food habits of the Amargosa pupfish in a thermal stream: Transactions of the American Fisheries Society, v. 104, p. 536–538.

Sada, D.W., 1990, Recovery plan for the endangered and threatened species of Ash Meadows, Nevada: Reno, Nevada, U.S. Fish and Wildlife Service.

Scoppettone, G.G., 1993, Interactions between native and nonnative fishes of upper Muddy River, Nevada: Transactions of the American Fisheries Society, v. 122, p. 599–608.

Scoppettone, G.G., Hereford, M.E., Rissler, P.H., Johnson, D.M., and Salgado, J.A., 2011, Relative abundance and distribution of fishes within an Established Area of Critical Environmental Concern, of the Amargosa Canyon and Willow Creek, Inyo and San Bernardino Counties, California: U.S. Geological Survey Open-File Report 2011-1061, 32 p.

Scoppettone, G.G., Rissler, P.H., Gourley, C., and Martinez, C., 2005, Habitat restoration as a means of controlling non-native fish in a Mojave Desert Oasis: Restoration Ecology, v. 13, p. 247–256.

Scoppettone, G.G., Rissler, P.H., Byers, S., Shea, S., Nielsen, B., and Sjoberg, J., 1995, Information on the status and ecology of Ash Meadows Fishes and *Ambrysus*: National Biological Service, Reno Field Station, 111 p.

Scoppettone, G.G., Rissler, P.H., Johnson, D., and Hereford, M., 2011, Relative abundance and distribution of fishes and crayfish at Ash Meadows National Wildlife Refuge, Nye County, Nevada, 2007–08: U.S. Geological Survey Open-File Report 2011-1017, 56 p.

Soltz, K.L., and Naiman, R.J., 1978, The natural history of native fishes in the Death Valley system: Natural History Museum of Los Angeles County, California, Science Series, v. 30, 76 p.

St. George, D., 1999, Ash Meadows National Wildlife Refuge nonnative fishes eradication report 1998: Ash Meadows National Wildlife Refuge, Nevada, 4 p.

Weissenfluh, D., 2008, Ash Meadows NWR aquatic exotic control activities summary accomplish report (FY 2008): U.S. Fish and Wildlife Service, 9 p.

Weissenfluh, D., 2011, Eradication of sailfin molly (*Poecilia latipinna*) from the Longstreet Spring System, Ash Meadows National Wildlife Refuge, Nevada Report: U.S. Fish and Wildlife Service, 10 p.

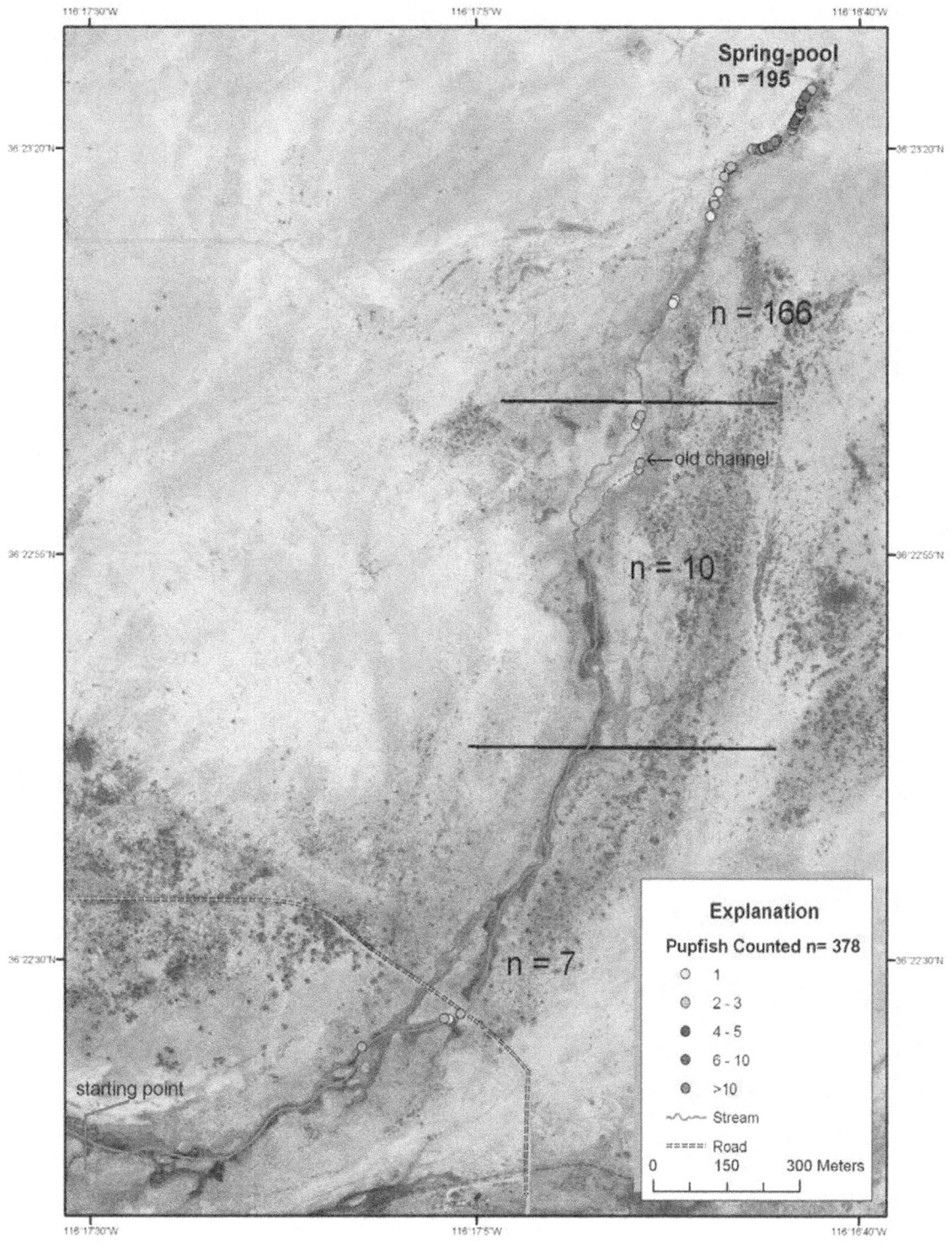

Figure 2.1. March 2006 distribution and relative abundance of Ash Meadow pupfish in the upper 2.25 km of the Jackrabbit Spring system. The stream image is divided into three equidistant strata, with number (n) of fish in each strata and in the spring-pool.

25

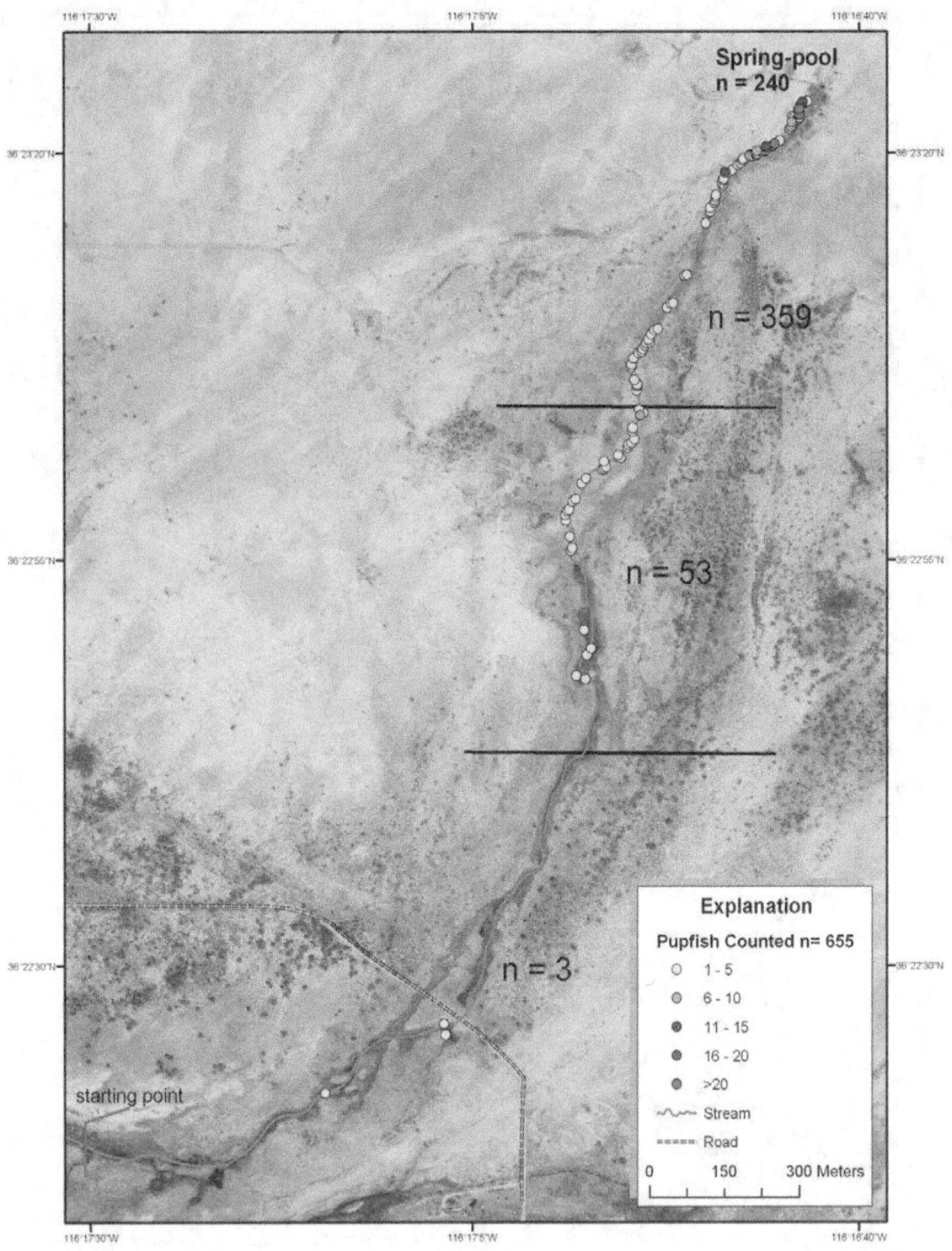

Figure 2.2. March 2007 distribution and relative abundance of Ash Meadow pupfish in the upper 2.25 km of the Jackrabbit Spring system. The stream image is divided into three equidistant strata, with number (n) of fish in each strata and in the spring-pool.

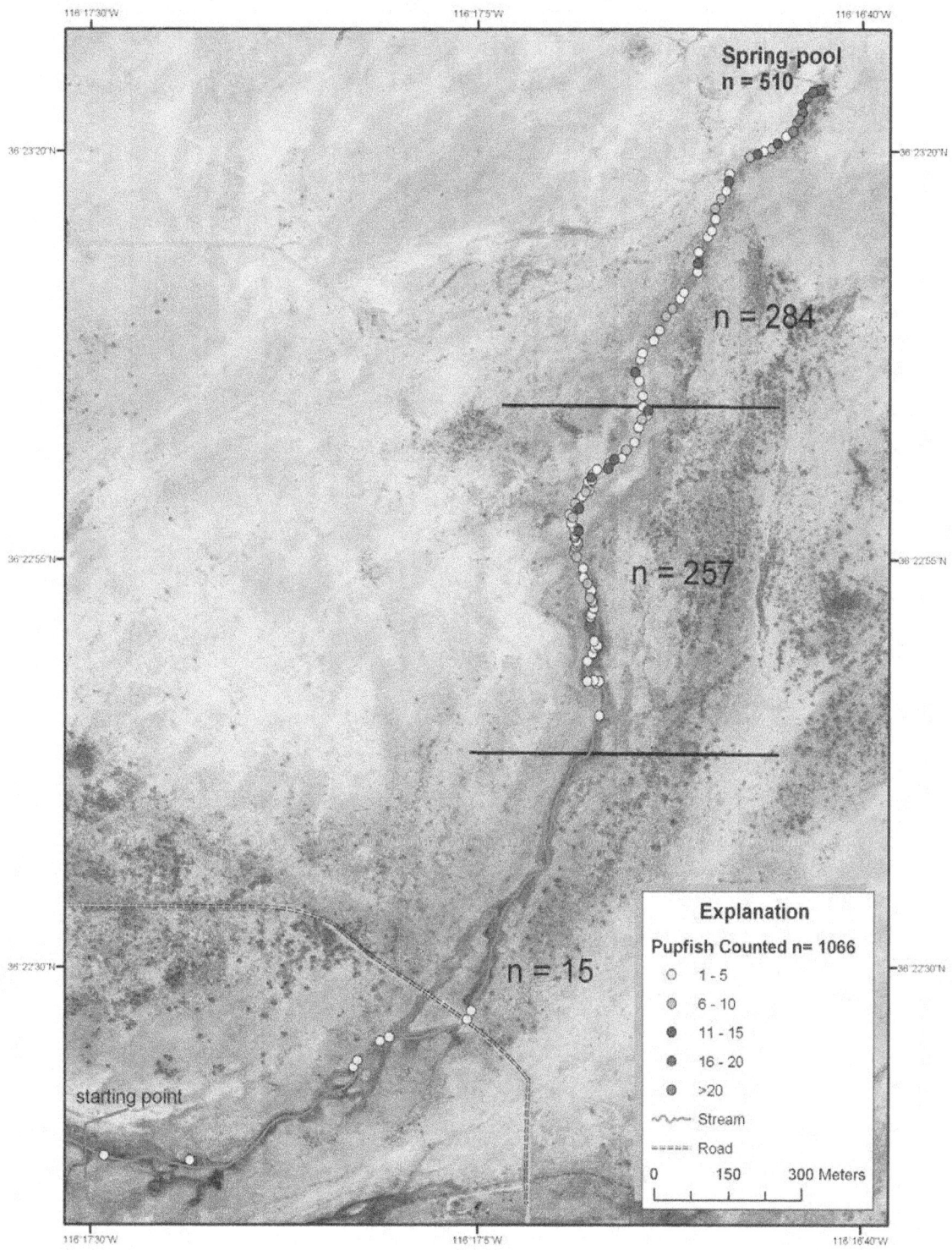

Figure 2.3. March 2010 distribution and relative abundance of Ash Meadow pupfish in the upper 2.25 km of the Jackrabbit Spring system. The stream image is divided into three equidistant strata with number (n) of fish in each strata and in the spring-pool.

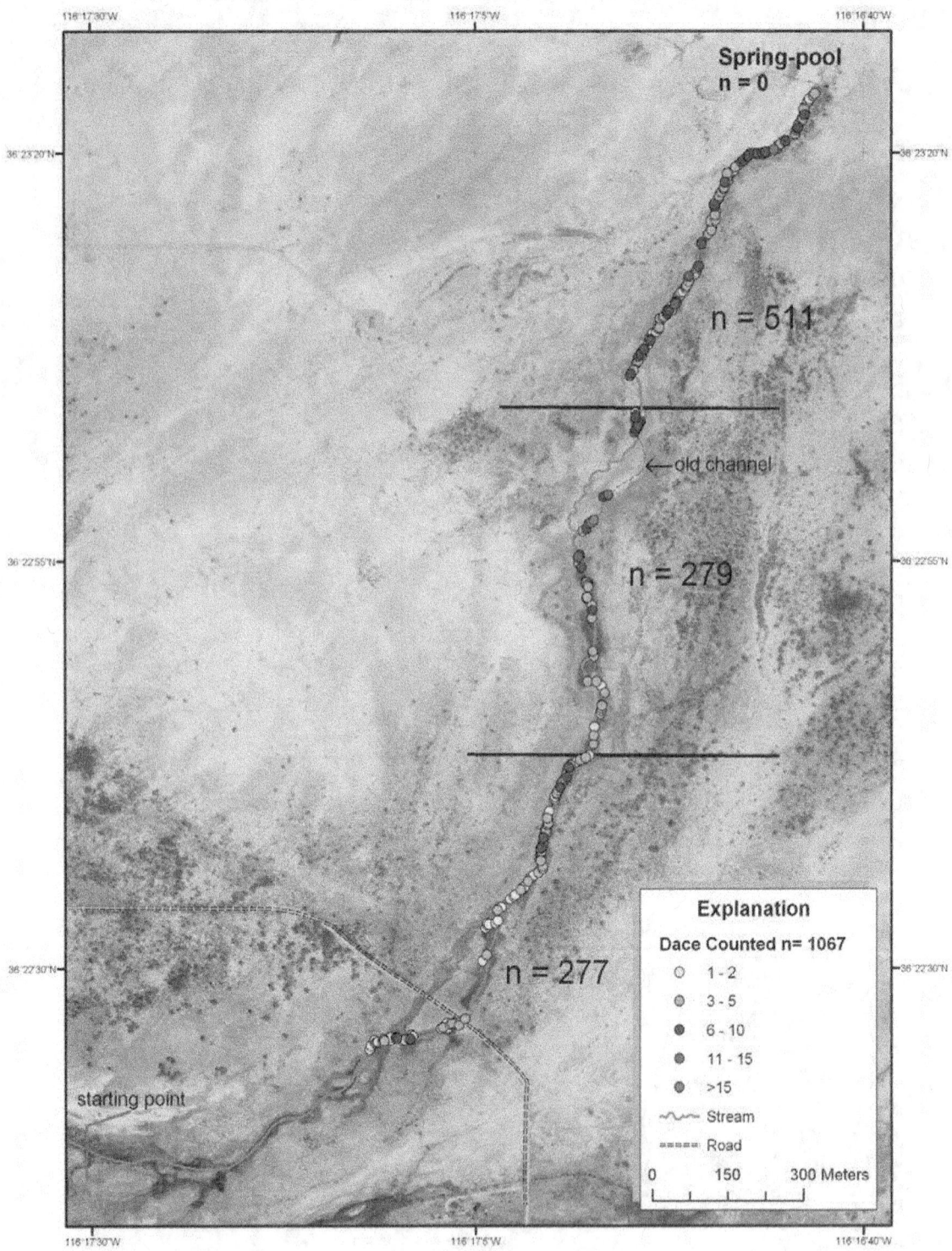

Figure 2.4. March 2006 distribution and relative abundance of Ash Meadow speckled dace in the upper 2.25 km of the Jackrabbit Spring system. The stream image is divided into three equidistant strata, with number (n) of fish in each strata and in the spring-pool.

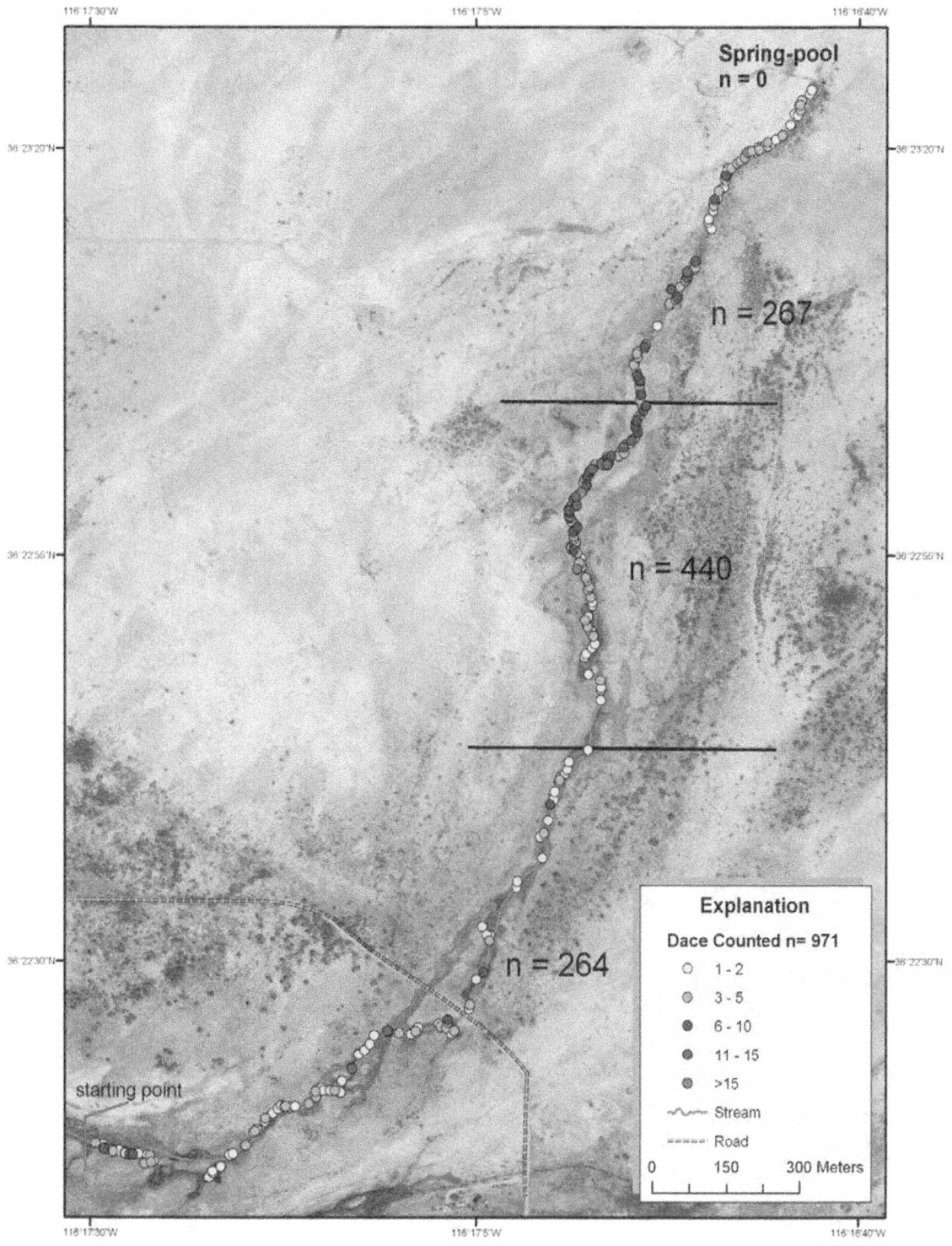

Figure 2.5. March 2007 distribution and relative abundance of Ash Meadow speckled dace in the upper 2.25 km of the Jackrabbit Spring system. The stream image is divided into three equidistant strata, with number (n) of fish in each strata and in the spring-pool.

29

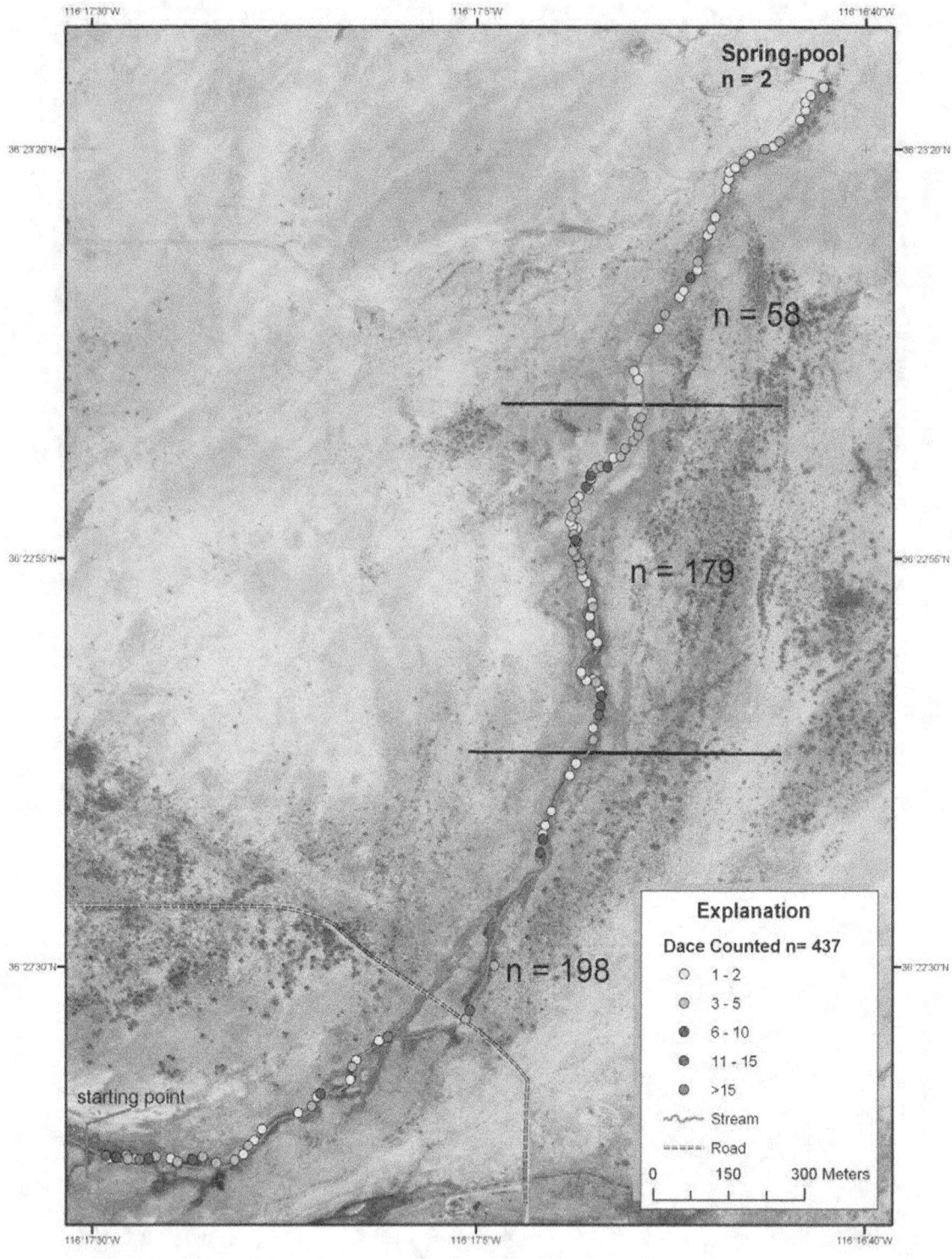

Figure 2.6. March 2010 distribution and relative abundance of Ash Meadow speckled dace in the upper 2.25 km of the Jackrabbit Spring system. The stream image is divided into three equidistant strata, with number (n) of fish in each strata and in the spring-pool.

30

Shallow Marsh Habitat Use by Amargosa Ash Meadows and Amargosa Warm Springs Pupfish

By Danielle M. Johnson, Mark E. Hereford, Peter H. Rissler, and G. Gary Scoppettone, U.S. Geological Survey

Ash Meadows National Wildlife Refuge (AMNWR) harbors two of the five extant subspecies of Amargosa pupfish (Miller, 1948), the Ash Meadows Amargosa pupfish (*Cyprinodon nevadensis mionectes*), and the Warm Springs Amargosa pupfish (*Cyprinodon nevadensis pectoralis*), both of which are federally listed as endangered (U.S. Fish and Wildlife Service, 1983). To improve the status of these fishes, the spring systems they inhabit are being restored. Ash Meadows spring systems typically include a spring-pool from which the spring emanates; a spring-brook discharging from the spring-pool, and marsh habitat at the spring-system terminus. Habitat conducive to Amargosa pupfish has been studied for spring-pools and spring-brooks (Scoppettone and others, 1995, 2005), while less information exists for marshes.

A comprehensive survey suggested Amargosa pupfish were widespread throughout Ash Meadows (Scoppettone and others, 2011), but that their number was substantially greater in specific habitat types. In marsh habitat, the largest number of pupfish were captured in more open-water marshes with sparse vegetative growth, while substantially fewer captures of pupfish typically occurred in dense stands of cattails (*Typha* spp.). Determining which habitat is conducive to native fishes is important when planning and executing habitat restoration. In this study, we test pupfish abundance in terms of marsh habitat type.

Marsh habitat occupies more than 50 percent of Ash Meadows surface water, and is primarily comprised of two vegetative communities (*Typha* or *Juncus* spp.). Our focus in this study was shallow water (less than 500 mm) marshes, because they are easier to control and manipulate than an expansive deep water marsh. The deep-water, marsh-like habitats of Ash Meadows also are occupied by non-native largemouth bass (*Micropterus salmoides*) and green sunfish (*Lepomis cyanellus*), predators incompatible to pupfish persistence.

Background

Historically, Ash Meadows' larger spring systems discharged into a common channel (Carson Slough) and thence the Amargosa River (Miller, 1948). Major alteration in the 1960s and 1970s associated with the development of Ash Meadows and its spring system for agriculture led to spring-system alteration and fragmentation (Pister, 1974; Soltz and Naiman, 1978; Sada, 1990; Deacon and Williams, 1991). Water was conveyed in earthen and concrete-lined ditches, or pumped from the spring-source (Pister, 1974).

Ash Meadows also has had a long history of non-native species introductions. Non-native western mosquitofish (*Gambusia affinis*), American bullfrog (*Lethobates catesbeiana*), and red-swamp crayfish (*Procambarus clarki*) inhabited Ash Meadows spring systems when spring systems were sampled in the 1930s (Miller, 1948). An endeavor to rear tropical freshwater fishes commercially in an Ash Meadows spring system released several fish invaders into Ash Meadows aquatic habitats in the 1960s (Soltz and Naiman, 1978), but only the sailfin molly (*Poecilia lapinna*) successfully established itself during that early enterprise and still persisted at the time of this study.

Materials and Methods

Twenty sampling sites were established in marsh habitat throughout Ash Meadows; 10 sites in *Typha* and 10 in *Juncus* marsh (fig. 3.1). Sites were sampled seasonally from July 2009 through April 2010 using standard Gee minnow traps (3.3 mm mesh). At sites with water equal to or less than 120 mm in depth, we used fabricated traps, described by Scoppettone and others (2011), 90 mm in width and also having a 3.3 mm mesh. Traps were baited with dry dog food and fished overnight. Captured fish were identified by species and enumerated, and 10 individuals were randomly selected for fork-length measurements. Vegetation and substrate surveys were conducted at each station. We used analysis of variance to test for a difference in number of pupfish captured between *Typha* and *Juncus* marshes. To satisfy conditions of normality and homogeneity, data were subjected to square root transformation. We also tested vegetation cover, water depth, and temperature between the two types of vegetative marshes. Vegetative cover was estimated by judging what percentage of the sample site was occupied by vegetation. Depth measurements were from water surface to marsh bottom, and water temperature was taken with a pocket thermometer. We used analysis of variance to test differences for each of the habitat conditions. Relative percent cover among sites was arc sin transformed, and depth was natural log transformed to improve normality and homogeneity.

We used a single-season, multi-state occupancy model in Program Mark (White and Burnham, 1999; Hewitt and others, 2008) to determine if there were differences between pupfish densities in *Typha* and *Juncus* marshes. We counted the number of fish captured by species for each site. Pupfish captures were divided into three abundance categories as follows: absent (no pupfish captured); low density (1-9 pupfish captured); and high density (equal to or greater than 10 pupfish captured). We also measured water depth, water temperature, dissolved oxygen, conductivity, pH, and estimated percentage of vegetation cover at each site. We ranked results from candidate models using Akaike's information criterion adjusted for small sample size (AIC_c), and used model averaging to obtain parameter estimates (Burnham and Anderson, 2002).

Results

Pupfish were captured from *Juncus* marshes in greater frequency than *Typha* marshes (fig. 3.2); there was a mean of 28 pupfish captured per site, while *Typha* had a mean of 4 pupfish captured per site, and this difference was significant (df = 1,18; F = 8.13; P = 0.011). Almost three times as many western mosquitofish, and twice the number of red swamp crayfish, were captured from *Typha* marshes than were captured from *Juncus* marshes; however, mosquitofish and crayfish captures outnumbered pupfish even in *Juncus* marshes. There was no significant difference in the number of crayfish (df = 1,18; F = 1.102; P = 0.308) or mosquitofish (df =1,18; F = 0.916 P = 0.351) between the two marsh types. The lowest captures for pupfish, mosquitofish, and crayfish were in winter (fig. A.1), but the greatest capture for pupfish was in spring, mosquitofish was in summer, and crayfish was in fall.

Mean cover at *Typha* marshes was 81 percent compared to 50 percent at *Juncus* marsh sites, and this difference was significant (df = 1,18; F = 7.242; p = 0.015). Mean water depth was 193 mm at *Typha* sites compared to 89 mm at *Juncus* sites, and this difference was significant (df = 1,18; F = 8.419; P = 0.010). Mean water temperature was slightly higher (24.1° C) at *Juncus* sites than *Typha* (22.9° C), but this difference was not significant (df = 1,18; F = 1.451; p = 0.244).

The best model included both marsh type and crayfish density in estimating pupfish occupancy (ψ 1), but model weight (ω) was relatively low (0.22), indicating little separation from competing models. The marsh type was important in 12 of the top 17 models, with a combined model weight of 0.79 indicating that marsh type is important to pupfish distribution (table 3.1). Of the site covariates, only crayfish and mosquitofish density had weight, but these were low compared to marsh vegetative type.

Discussion

The *Juncus* marsh community supported a significantly greater density of Amargosa pupfish than the shallow *Typha* marsh community. Among *Juncus* marshes, there was significantly greater open-water habitat, allowing greater sunlight exposure, and presumably increased algae growth, which is important forage for Amargosa pupfish (Naiman, 1975). Shallow *Typha* marshes were densely vegetated, with the plants eight to ten times higher than *Juncus,* creating areas of 100 percent cover. Solar radiation in open waters presumably provides water temperatures warm enough for pupfish reproduction (Soltz and Niaman, 1978); however, our spot temperature measurements were insufficient to evaluate temperate suitability between the two marsh habitat types. Another possible advantage of the shallow open-water marsh is the occurrence of fewer invasive mosquitofish and crayfish, both of which have been proven to impact native fishes negatively (Courtenay and Meffe, 1989; Freeman and others, 2010; Larson and Olden, 2011).

Red swamp crayfish that feed on a wide array of food stuffs (Whiteledge and Rabeni, 1997; Kennedy and others, 2006) were captured with greater frequency in the *Typha* marsh community than the *Juncus* community. Western mosquitofish also were captured with greater frequency in the *Typha* community. Although these invasive species were captured in twice the numbers in *Typha* than *Juncus*, the difference was not significant and may have been due to our small sample size.

Again, we suspect that open water is an important habitat component affecting Amargosa pupfish abundance in shallow marsh habitat, and an important consideration in developing shallow marsh habitat on the AMNWR. Water availability typically is the primary driving force in plant distribution and abundance, and might be an important focus when developing shallow marsh habitat. For example, *Juncus* generally has a fairly extensive root system, and can thrive in areas of high groundwater (Mata-González and others, 2012). When surface water is the primary water source, we have observed water shifting when *Juncus* becomes dense enough to deflect streamflow (Point of Rocks Marsh, and South Scruggs Marsh); this dynamic is especially true on flat terrain. Thus, selecting flat over entrenched terrain for the development of shallow marsh habitat may enhance opportunity for greater open-water habitat by allowing the marsh to shift as emergent vegetation thickens. This dynamic also has a secondary effect of restricting the establishment of *Typha*, which thrives in permanently boggy habitat.

Rehabilitating marsh habitat most conducive to Amargosa pupfish probably is most important in low-water-volume systems offering little to no spring-pool habitat, and only modest pupfish habitat availability in the spring-brook. More open-water marsh habitat may offer a substantial portion of pupfish habitat in such low-water-volume systems as occur in the Warm Springs complex, and Soda and Cold Springs. Marsh habitat probably is important habitat in Ash Meadows' more cool-water springs (Bradford 1, Bradford 2, and Cold Spring). Because water discharged from these springs at temperatures well below the 26°C required for pupfish reproduction, open marsh habitat with water temperatures influenced by ambient air temperature and solar radiation may become important reproductive habitat in these cool-water systems.

References Cited

Burnham, K.P., and Anderson, D.R., 2002, Model selection and multi-model inference—Practical information-theoretic approach: New York, Springer Science Business Media, 514 p.

Courtenay, W.R., Jr. and Meffe, G.K., 1989, Small fishes in strange places—A review of introduced poeciliids, *in* Meffe, G.K., and Snelson, Jr., F.F., eds., Ecology and evolution of livebearing fishes (Poeciliidae): Englewood Cliffs, New Jersey, Prentice Hall, p. 319–331

Deacon, J.E., and Williams, C.D., 1991, Ash Meadows and the legacy of Devils Hole pupfish, *in* Minckley, W.L., and Deacon, J.E., eds., Battle against extinction—Native fish management in the American West: Tucson, The University of Arizona Press, p. 69–87.

Freeman, M.A., Turnbull, J.F., Yeomans, W.E., and Bean, C.W., 2010, Prospects for management strategies of invasive crayfish populations with an emphasis on biological control, Aquatic Conservation: Marine and Freshwater Ecosystems, v. 20, p. 211–223.

Hewitt, D.A., Fabrizio, M.C., Hewitt, A.H., and Ellis, J.K., 2008, Habitat selection by juvenile striped bass in lower Chesapeake Bay tributaries—Inferences from occupancy models: Gloucester Point, Virginia, Virginia Institute of Marine Science, Department of Fisheries Science, Final Report for NOAA Award NA04NMF4570375.

Kennedy, T.A., Finlay, J.C., and Hobbie, S.E., 2006, Eradication of invasive *Tamarix ramosissima* along a desert stream increases native fish density: Ecological Application v. 15, p. 2,072–2,083.

Larson, E.R., and Olden, J.D., 2011, The state of crayfish in the Pacific Northwest: Fisheries, v. 36, no. 2, v. 61–73.

Mata-González, R., McLendon, T., Marin, D.W., Trilica, M.J., and Pearce, R.A., 2012, Vegetation as affected by groundwater depth and microtopography in a shallow aquifer area of the Great Basin: Ecohydrology, v. 5, p. 54–63.

Miller, R.R., 1948, The cyprinodont fishes of the Death Valley system of eastern California and southeastern California and southeastern Nevada: University of Michigan, Miscellaneous publications of the Museum of Zoology, v. 68, p. 1–155.

Naiman, R.J., 1975, Food habits of the Amargosa pupfish in a thermal stream: Transaction of the American Fisheries Society, v. 104, p. 536–538.

Pister, E.P., 1974, Desert fishes and their habitats: Transactions of the American Fisheries Society, v. 103, p. 531–540.

Sada, D.W., 1990, Recovery plan for the endangered and threatened species of Ash Meadows, Nevada: Reno, Nevada, U.S. Fish and Wildlife Service.

Scoppettone, G.G., Rissler, P.H., Byers, S., Shea, S., Nielsen, B., and Sjöberg, J., 1995, Information on the status and ecology of Ash Meadows Fishes and *Ambrysus*: National Biological Service, Reno Field Station, 111 p.

Scoppettone, G.G., Rissler, P.H., Gourley, C., and Martinez, C., 2005, Habitat restoration as a means of controlling non-native fish in a Mojave Desert Oasis, Restoration Ecology, v. 13, p. 247-256.

Scoppettone, G.G., Rissler, P.H., Johnson, D., and Hereford, M., 2011, Relative abundance and distribution of fishes and crayfish at Ash Meadows National Wildlife Refuge, Nye County, Nevada, 2007-08: U.S. Geological Survey Open-File Report 2011-1017, 56 p.

Soltz, K.L. and Naiman, R.J., 1978, The natural history of native fishes in the Death Valley system: Natural History Museum of Los Angeles County, California, Science Series, 76 p.

U.S. Fish and Wildlife Service, 1983, Endangered and threatened wildlife and plants determination of endangered status and critical habitats for two fish species in Ash Meadows, Nevada, Federal Register, v. 48, p. 40178-40186.

White, G.C. and Burnham, K.P., 1999, Program MARK: survival estimation from populations of marked animals, Bird Study 46 Supplement, p. 120-138.

Whiteledge, G.W. and Rabeni, C.F., 1997, Energy sources and ecological role of crayfish in an Ozark stream: insights from stable isotopes and gut analysis, Canadian Journal of Aquatic Sciences, v. 54, p. 2555-2563.

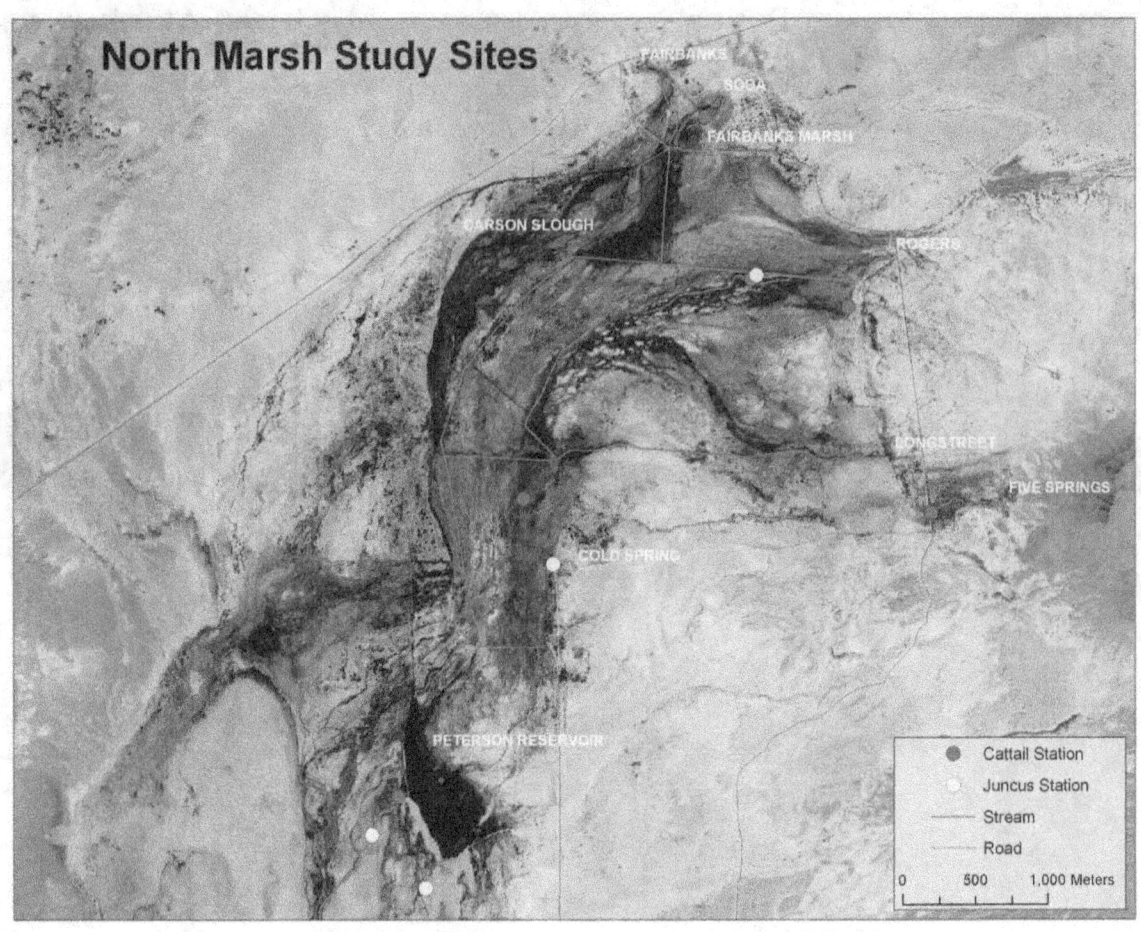

Figure 3.1. Study sites at the Northern and Southern spring systems at Ash Meadows National Wildlife Refuge.

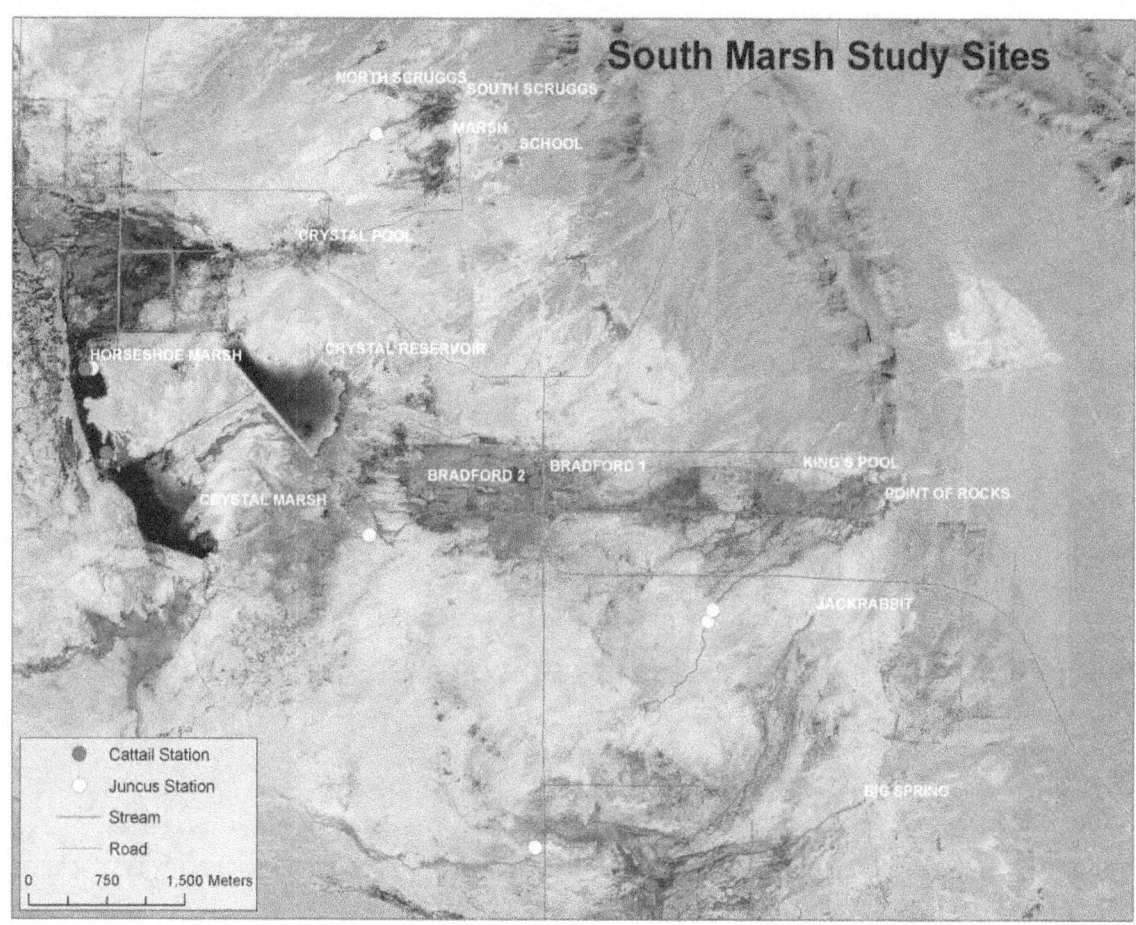

Figure 3.1. Study sites at the Northern and Southern spring systems at Ash Meadows National Wildlife Refuge.—Continued

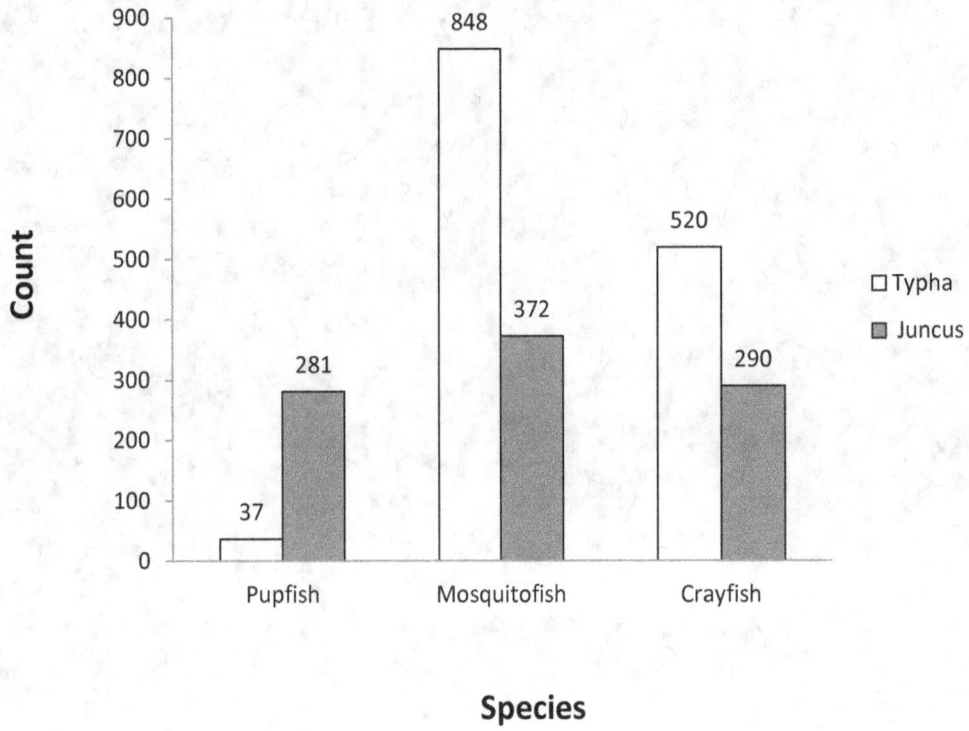

Figure 3.2. Total number of Amargosa pupfish, western mosquitofish, and red swamp crayfish captured from *Typha* and *Juncus* marshes in four seasons, 2009 and 2010.

Table 3.1. Values of the Akaike's information criterion corrected for small sample size used to select the best model from 53 candidate models of marsh occupancy during 2009-10 (the top 17 models are shown). A period (.) indicates that the parameter is constant over that attribute; x denotes full model, + denotes an additive model. The best model (lowest AICc value) is presented first; ΔAICc is the difference between AICc values of the individual models and that of the best model. Akaike weights (ω) provide a measure of each model's relative weight or likelihood of being the best model in the data set given. Number of parameters (K) is the total number that is theoretically estimable by the model.

Model[a]	AIC_c	ΔAIC_c	ω	K
ψ1(marsh x CFden) ψ2(.) p1(.) p2(.) δ(season)	135.82	0.00	0.22	7
ψ1(marsh) ψ2(.) p1(.) p2(.) δ(season)	136.19	0.37	0.18	7
ψ1(.) ψ2(.) p1(.) p2(.) δ(season)	137.25	1.44	0.11	6
ψ1(marsh x CFden) ψ2(.) p1(.) p2(.) δ(winter)	137.50	1.68	0.09	7
ψ1(marsh) ψ2(.) p1(.) p2(.) δ(winter)	137.88	2.06	0.08	7
ψ1(marsh x Gamden) ψ2(.) p1(.) p2(.) δ(season)	138.19	2.38	0.07	7
ψ1(marsh x CFden) ψ2(.) p1(.) p2(.) δ(.)	138.74	2.92	0.05	6
ψ1(marsh) ψ2(.) p1(.) p2(.) δ(.)	139.11	3.29	0.04	6
ψ1(marsh x Gamden) ψ2(.) p1(.) p2(.) δ(winter)	139.87	4.06	0.03	7
ψ1(.) ψ2(.) p1(.) p2(.) δ(.)	140.87	5.05	0.02	5
ψ1(Gamden) ψ2(.) p1(.) p2(.) δ(season)	141.36	5.54	0.01	7
ψ1(.) ψ2(.) p1(marsh) p2(.) δ(marsh)	141.79	5.97	0.01	7
ψ1(marsh) ψ2(.) p1(.) p2(.) δ(marsh + season)	141.89	6.07	0.01	8
ψ1(CFden) ψ2(.) p1(.) p2(.) δ(season)	141.93	6.11	0.01	7
ψ1(marsh) ψ2(marsh) p1(.) p2(.) δ(marsh)	142.39	6.57	0.01	7
ψ1(marsh x CFden) ψ2(.) p1(winter) p2(.) δ(winter)	142.48	6.66	0.01	8
ψ1(marsh) ψ2(.) p1(.) p2(.) δ(marsh)	142.56	6.74	0.01	7

[a] model variables represent ψ1 = probability that a site is occupied regardless of density; ψ2 = probability that a site has high density given that the site is occupied; p1 = probability that occupancy is detected for a site for a given time period given that it is actually occupied; p2 = probability that occupancy is detected for a site for a given time period given that it is actually occupied with high density; δ = probability that evidence of high density is found, given detection of occupancy at the site at a given time period; site covariates represent marsh = juncus or typha CFden = crayfish density; Gamden = mosquitofish density; season = summer, fall, winter, spring; winter = winter is separated from the other seasons.

Population Dynamics of Amargosa Ash Meadows Pupfish in Five Springs, Ash Meadows, Nye County Nevada

By G. Gary Scoppettone, Peter H. Rissler, Mark E. Hereford, and Danielle M. Johnson, U.S. Geological Survey

Management of any resource requires inventory and monitoring (LaRoe and others, 1995), and effective monitoring requires an understanding of species' seasonal population trends. Population size can be influenced by seasonal changes in biotic and abiotic conditions (Williams and others, 2002; Riggs and Deacon, 2003). In thermal-spring systems, such as Ash Meadows, many abiotic conditions (temperature, dissolved oxygen, flow, pH, and conductivity) remain fairly constant year round. Day length is an abiotic factor that does change, which in turn affects primary productivity (Naiman, 1976). The seasonal shift in pupfish population number as a result of primary productivity changes should be a consideration when evaluating relative population health.

Previous population estimates were based on spring-pool samples and conducted at various times of the year (Threloff, 1990; St. George, 1999). The spring-pools were sampled open systems with pupfish free to enter or leave the spring-pool via its outflow. Most Ash Meadows spring systems flow into marsh-like habitat, making it difficult to conduct seasonal population counts. The only pupfish population in Ash Meadows with numerical estimates of the entire population is Devils Hole pupfish (*Cyprinodon diabolis*) (Andersen and Deacon, 2001); because its habitat is sufficiently minute to facilitate annual and seasonal counts of the entire population. However, because it is a cavernous limnocrene and light-limited for much of the year, there have been wide swings in primary productivity and fish population numbers (Wilson and Blinn, 2007).

The Five Springs system is a complex that harbors Amargosa Ash Meadows pupfish (*Cyprinodon nevadensis mionectes*) and is sufficiently diminutive and easy to sample as a closed system. Its exposure to sunlight is more representative of Ash Meadow limnocrenes, and thus may serve as a model for population fluctuations in Ash Meadows spring systems.

Description of Area

Five Springs is located in Ash Meadows' northern springs, and is comprised of a series of small springs and seeps (Dudley and Larson, 1976). Situated just east of Longstreet Spring, Five Springs had a cumulative discharge of 617 L/min when measured by Dudley and Larson (1976). Situated at an elevation of 2,350 m, Five Springs complex is the highest of Ash Meadows springs. During this study, the discharges of the spring complex flowed into a single channel, and dissipated less than 140 m downstream of the highest spring. The spring complex is inhabited by two native spring snails (*Gastropoda: Hydrobiidae*) (Hershler and Sada, 1987) and the invasive red-rim melania (*Melonoides tuberculata*), red swamp crayfish (*Procambarus clarki*), and western mosquitofish (*Gambusia affinis*) (Scoppettone and others, 2011).

Materials and Methods

We estimated population numbers for adult pupfish (equal to or greater than 25 mm total length - TL) bimonthly in the Five Springs system from October 2009 to October 2010. We used modified minnow traps described by Scoppettone and others (2011) and set 38 traps in 37 locations; two standard Gee minnow traps with 3.3 mm mesh were set at Spring 6 because it was a large pool and harbored the majority of Five Springs pupfish. Baited with dry dog food, the minnow traps were spaced every 10 m throughout the Five Springs system. All pupfish were within 5 m of a baited minnow trap, and all were considered to have an equal capture probability. To reduce stress on captured fish, minnow traps were only set for 2 to 4 hours. Pupfish equal to or greater than 25 mm TL were marked by clipping the caudal fin. All fish were then released halfway between capture sites. From 1 to 3 days later, minnow traps were set in the same location and the number of unmarked and the marked adult fish was counted. We estimated the adult pupfish population using the Lincoln-Petersen estimator adjusted for sample size bias (Williams and others, 2002). We calculated 95 percent asymptotic confidence intervals as per Seber (1982). For length frequency analysis, we measured all pupfish captured on the first day of sampling. All fish were measured to the nearest 1 mm, and then grouped into 3 mm increments. At least one spring was detected to be quite warm so we set four HOBO® thermographs at four selected sites to determine if pupfish distribution might be affected by water temperature.

Results

Population Dynamics

Population estimates of adult pupfish ranged from 143 (April 2010) to 307 (October 2010) (fig. 4.1). Generally, population numbers were lower in winter and spring and higher in summer and fall. The number of adult pupfish captured shows relatively small changes between sampling times and may indicate that the Five Springs pupfish population is actually more stable than what is shown with the population estimates (fig. 4.1). We did not estimate population size of mosquitofish and crayfish, but compared capture trends with that of pupfish. Similar to pupfish, more mosquitofish were captured in the fall, but substantially less were captured in the spring. Crayfish captures were lowest in the fall and greatest in spring and summer.

Pupfish were captured at 24 of 37 stations during sampling (fig. 4.2). Fish were absent from the upper seven sampling stations of Spring 5 (fig. 4.2), which probably was due to warmer temperatures; water temperature ranged from 32.5 to 33.9° C ($\bar{x}$ = 32.9° C) 20 m downstream of the spring source. A HOBO® that was placed 120 m downstream of the spring sources had much greater daily and seasonal fluctuation (fig. 4.3). Captures at lower stations upstream of Spring 6 (fig. 4.2) occurred in the cooler months (November–April) when maximum water temperatures remained lower than 30° C. The greatest capture rate occurred at the large pool at Spring 6, accounting for 57 percent of the pupfish captured from the Five Springs system; seasonal and daily shift in temperature was greater in Spring 6 outflow than it was in the Spring 5 outflow. Spring 3 (fig. 4.2) was actually a well and not accessible to pupfish, while other downstream locations not directly on the Spring 5 discharge were very shallow high-gradient reaches that were difficult to trap effectively. Distribution of mosquitofish and crayfish was more restricted than pupfish; mosquitofish were captured at nine stations and crayfish at seven (figs. 4.4, 4.5).

The greatest mosquitofish capture rate was from traps set at a pool on Spring 6 accounting for 77 percent of the captures. One individual was captured at the source, where water temperature was nearly 33° C. The greatest capture success for crayfish was at the origin of Spring 2 (4.5) accounting for 43 percent of captures.

Mean total length of pupfish captured at Five Springs ranged from 26 to 29 mm TL, with August 2010 and October 2010 having the smallest mean size (fig. 4.6). Length frequencies suggest that reproduction may occur from late summer (August) through the winter (February), with little to no reproduction occurring in spring and early summer (April, June). The smallest pupfish (9–12 mm TL) were captured in December, February, August, and October.

Discussion

Five Springs pupfish demonstrated a similar population trend as the Devils Hole pupfish, with peak numbers occurring in fall and lowest numbers occurring in spring (Andersen and Deacon, 2001; Riggs and Deacon, 2003). Mosquitofish also displayed a similar spring trend, but with a wider swing from spring to fall than Ash Meadows pupfish and more similar to Devils Hole pupfish. Fluctuations in Amargosa pupfish numbers from fall to spring have been linked to day length and associated primary productivity (Naiman, 1976). Dramatic shifts in Devils Hole pupfish numbers have been linked to severe limitation in primary productivity due to light limitation within its cavernous environment. Mosquitofish in Five Springs probably are not as food limited as pupfish in Devils Hole, but like Devils Hole pupfish their life span is only about 1 year (Swanson and others, 1996; Moyle, 2002); Ash Meadows pupfish, however, can live for several years (Scoppettone and others, 1995) so a winter decline may not have a profound effect on the population. Crayfish numbers did not follow the trend of greatest numbers of individuals captured in fall and least in spring. This is not totally unexpected because their catholic diet may allow them to exploit a greater variety of carbon sources than pupfish or mosquitofish (Kennedy and others, 2006). Crayfish also are harder to capture when they burrow (Penn, 1943), but when burrowing may occur in Ash Meadows has not been studied.

Consistent with the low discharge (less than 3.0 L/sec) springs situated higher (greater than 2,320 m) in Ash Meadows (Warm Springs complex and Point of Rocks complex), contributors to the Five Springs complex are quite warm, and these warm temperatures appear to influence pupfish distribution. The greatest concentration of pupfish occurred in the Spring 6 pool. Water temperature in the pool generally was favorable for pupfish, and the pool was sufficiently large that it probably offered a variety of temperate micro-climates even during the very warm summer (Nielsen and others, 1994). Although our HOBO® reported very warm summer temperatures, we suspect there were localized areas of hospitable temperature, sufficient to permit summertime reproduction.

Mosquitofish and crayfish negatively impact native fish populations (Swanson and others, 1996; Whitledge and Rabeni, 1997), but to what degree the pupfish population is suppressed by these species in Five Springs is unknown. However, the Five Springs complex is sufficiently restricted that it may be feasible to eradicate these two invaders from the system. Once these species are eliminated, data from this study can be used to gauge the effect that their removal has on the pupfish population. Five Springs is scientifically interesting because it offers low-water-volume thermal-springs habitat qualities quite similar to the Warm Springs complex.

Cursory morphological inspection of Five Spring pupfish suggests some degree of convergent evolution with Warm Springs pupfish (*Cyprinodon nevadensis pectoralis*). Similar to Warm Springs pupfish (Miller, 1948), the pelvic fins of Five Springs pupfish appear to be vestigial. The isolated Five Spring's population of Amargosa Ash Meadows pupfish requires protection and management to ensure its persistence.

Acknowledgments

We thank Ash Meadows National Wildlife Refuge for funding this project. We also thank Tom Strekal (Bureau of Indian Affairs, retired) and Mark Fabes (U.S. Geological Survey) for their critical review.

References Cited

Andersen, M.E., and Deacon, J.E., 2001, Population size of Devils Hole pupfish (*Cyprinodon diabolis*) correlates with water level: Copeia, p. 224–228.

Dudley, W.W., and Larson, J.D., 1976, Effect of irrigation pumping on desert pupfish habitat in Ash Meadows, Nye County, Nevada: U.S. Geological Survey Professional Paper 927, 52 p.

Hershler, R., and Sada, D.W., 1987, Springsnails (Gastropoda: Hydrobiidae) of Ash Meadows, Amargosa Basin, California-Nevada, Proceedings: Proceedings of the Biological Society of Washington, v. 100, p. 776–843.

Kennedy, T.A., Finlay, J.C., and Hobbie, S.E., 2006, Eradication on invasive *Tamarix ramosissima* along a desert stream increases native fish density: Ecological Application, v. 15, p. 2,072–2,083.

LaRoe, E.T., Farris, G.S., Puckett, C.E., Doran, P.D., and Mac, M.J., 1995, Our living resources—A report to the Nation on the distribution, abundance, and health of U.S. plants, animals, and ecosystems: U.S. Department of the Interior, National Biological Service, Washington, D.C., 530 p.

Miller, R.R., 1948, The cyprinodont fishes of the Death Valley System of eastern California and Southwestern Nevada: University of Michigan, Miscellaneous Publications Museum of Zoology, v. 68, 155 p.

Moyle, P.B., 2002, Inland fishes of California: Barkeley, University of California Press, 502 p.

Naiman, R. J., 1976, Productivity of a herbivorous pupfish population (*Cyrinodon nevadensis*) in a warm water desert stream: Journal of Fish Biology, v. 9, p. 125–137.

Nielsen, J.L., Lisle, T.E., and Ozarki, V., 1994, Thermal stratified pools and their use by steelhead in Northern California Streams: Transactions of the American Fisheries Society, v. 123, p. 613–626.

Penn, G.H., Jr., 1943, A Study of the life history of the Louisiana red-crawfish, *Cambarus clarkii* Girard: Ecology, v. 24, p. 1–18.

Riggs, A.C., and Deacon, J.E., 2003, Connectivity in desert aquatic ecosystems—The Devils Hole story, *in* Sada, D.W., and Sharpe, S.E., eds., Spring-fed wetlands—Important scientific and cultural resources of the Intermountain Region, Las Vegas, Nevada, May 7–9, 2002, Proceedings: DHS Publication No. 41210, p. 1–38, accessed December 31, 2012, at http://www.wetlands.dri.edu.

Scoppettone, G.G., Rissler, P.H., Byers, S., Shea, S., Nielsen, B., and Sjöberg, J., 1995, Information on the status and ecology of Ash Meadows Fishes and *Ambrysus*: National Biological Service, Reno Field Station, 111 p.

Scoppettone, G.G., Rissler, P., Johnson, D., and Hereford, M., 2011, Relative abundance and distribution of fishes and crayfish at Ash Meadows National Wildlife Refuge, Nye County, Nevada, 2007-08: U.S. Geological Survey Open-File Report 2011-1017, 56 p.

Seber, G.A.F., 1982, The estimation of animal abundance and related parameters: New York, New York, MacMillan, 506 p.

St. George, D., 1999, Ash Meadows National Wildlife Refuge 1998 native fish survey—Ash Meadows National Wildlife Refuge: U.S. Fish and Wildlife Service, 7 p.

Swanson, C., Cech, J.J., Jr., and Piedrahita, R.H., 1996, Mosquitofish biology, culture and use in mosquito control: Mosquito and Vector Control Association of California and The University of California Mosquito Research Program, 88 p.

Threloff, D., 1990, Ash Meadows biannual fish count summary—Ash Meadows National Wildlife Refuge: U.S. Fish and Wildlife Service, 11 p.

Whitledge, G.W., and Rabeni, C.F., 1997, Energy sources and ecological role of crayfishes in an Ozaek stream—Insights from stable isotopes and gut analysis: Canadian Journal of Aquatic Sciences, v. 54, p. 2,555–2,563.

Williams, B.K., J.D., Nichols, and Conroy, M.J., 2002, Analysis and management of animal populations—Modeling, estimation and decision making: San Diego, California, Academic Press, 817 p.

Wilson, K.P., and Blinn, D.W., 2007, Food Web structure energetic, and importance of allochthonous carbon in a desert cavernous limnocrene: Devils Hole, Nevada, v. 67, p. 185–198.

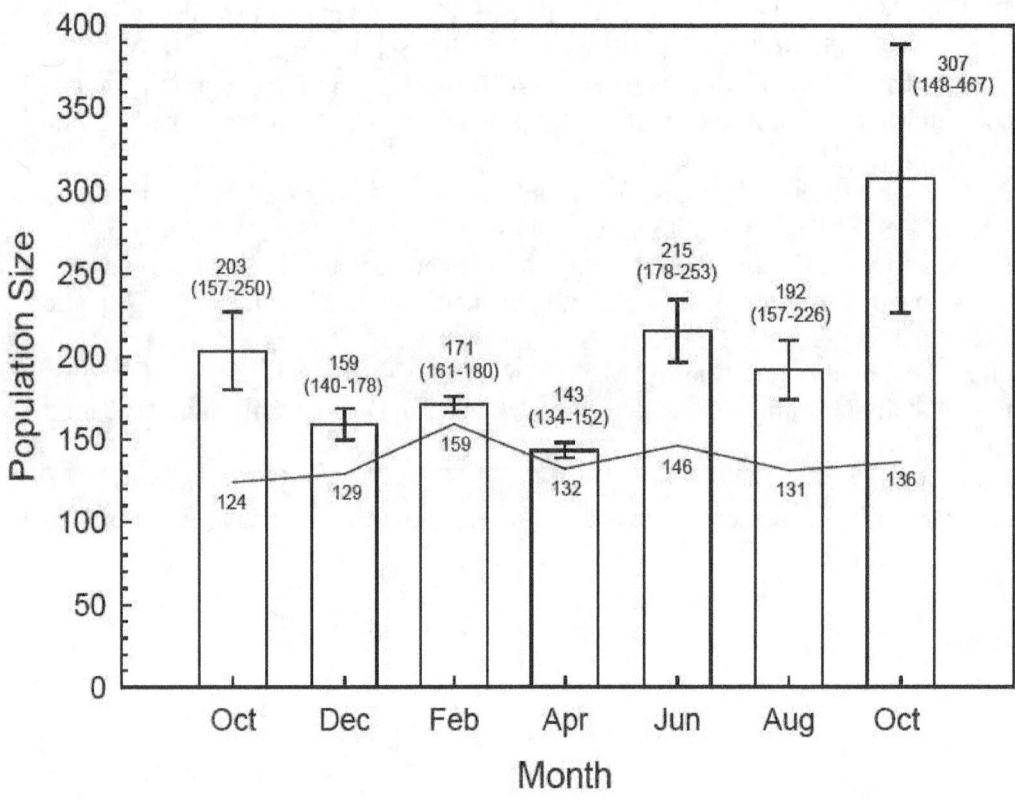

Figure 4.1. Bimonthly population estimate (bar graph) and confidence interval of Ash Meadows pupfish in Five Springs from October 2009 to October 2010. The line graph is bimonthly capture of unmarked pupfish. Only pupfish equal to or greater than 26 mm total length were used for bimonthly population estimate and total unmarked pupfish captured.

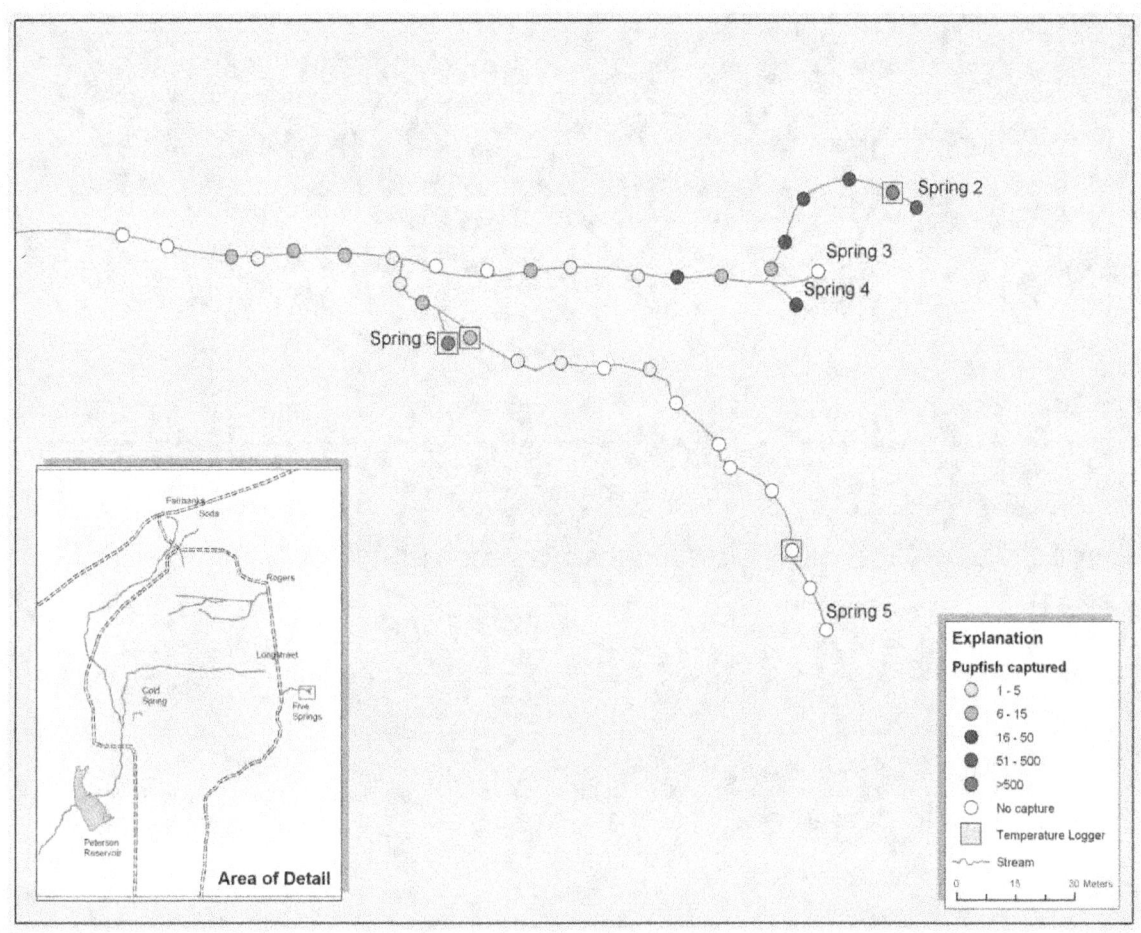

Figure 4.2. Ash Meadows pupfish distribution and relative abundance within the Five Springs system; captures are a composite of bimonthly sampling from October 2009 to October 2010. The four stations with a recording thermograph (HOBO®) are represented by a square symbol around the circular station.

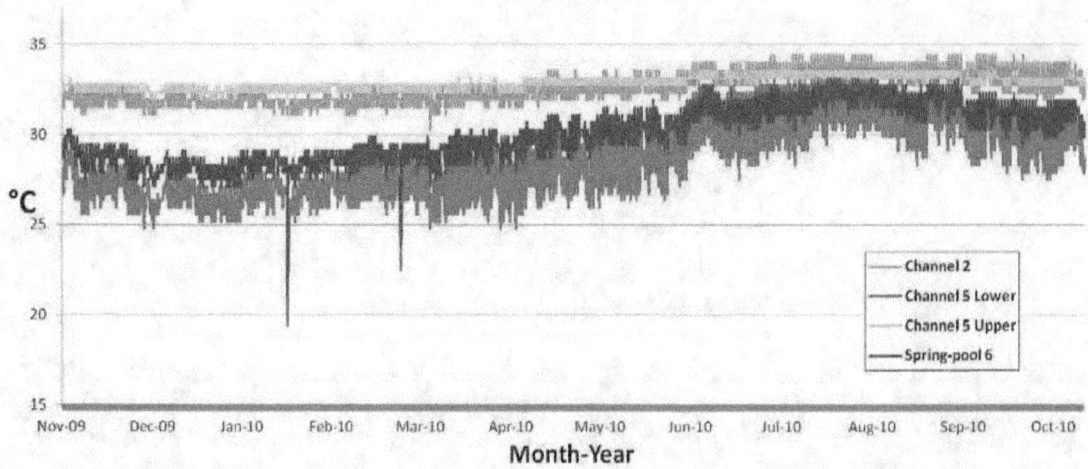

Figure 4.3. Daily HOBO® temperature record at four locations within the Five Springs system.

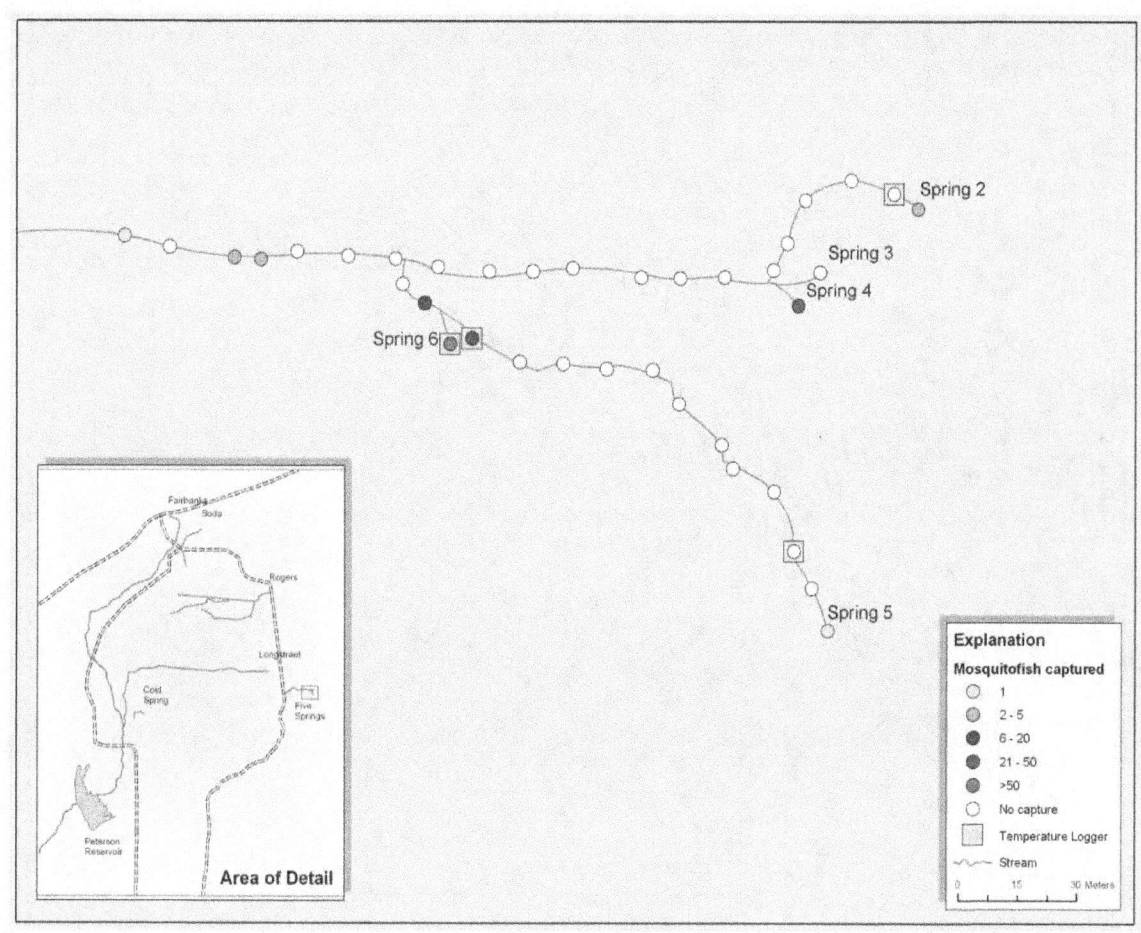

Figure 4.4. Western mosquitofish distribution and relative abundance within the Five Springs system; captures are a composite of bimonthly sampling from October 2009 to October 2010. The four stations with a recording thermograph (HOBO®) are represented by a square symbol round the circular station.

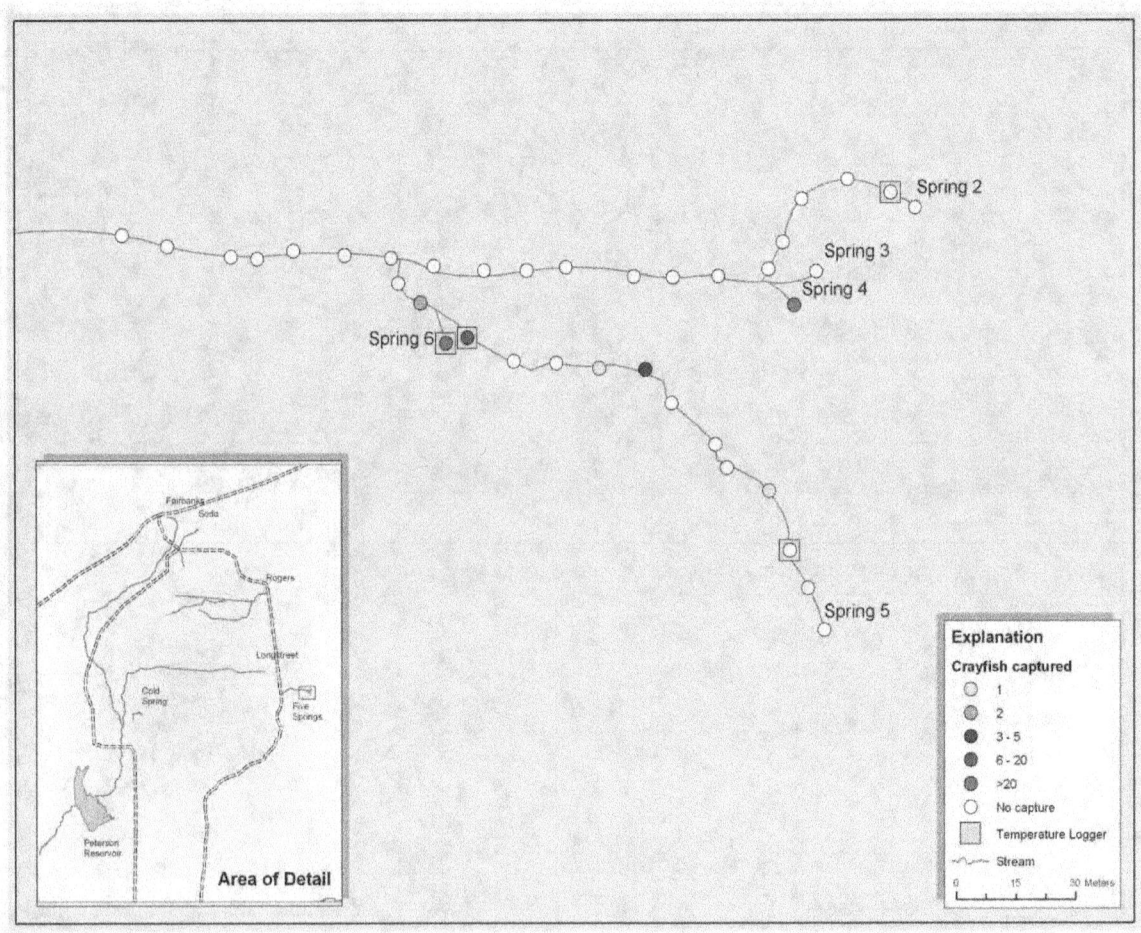

Figure 4.5. Red swamp crayfish distribution and relative abundance within the Five Springs system; captures are a composite of bimonthly sampling from October 2009 to October 2010. The four stations with a recording thermograph (HOBO®) are represented by a square symbol round the circular station.

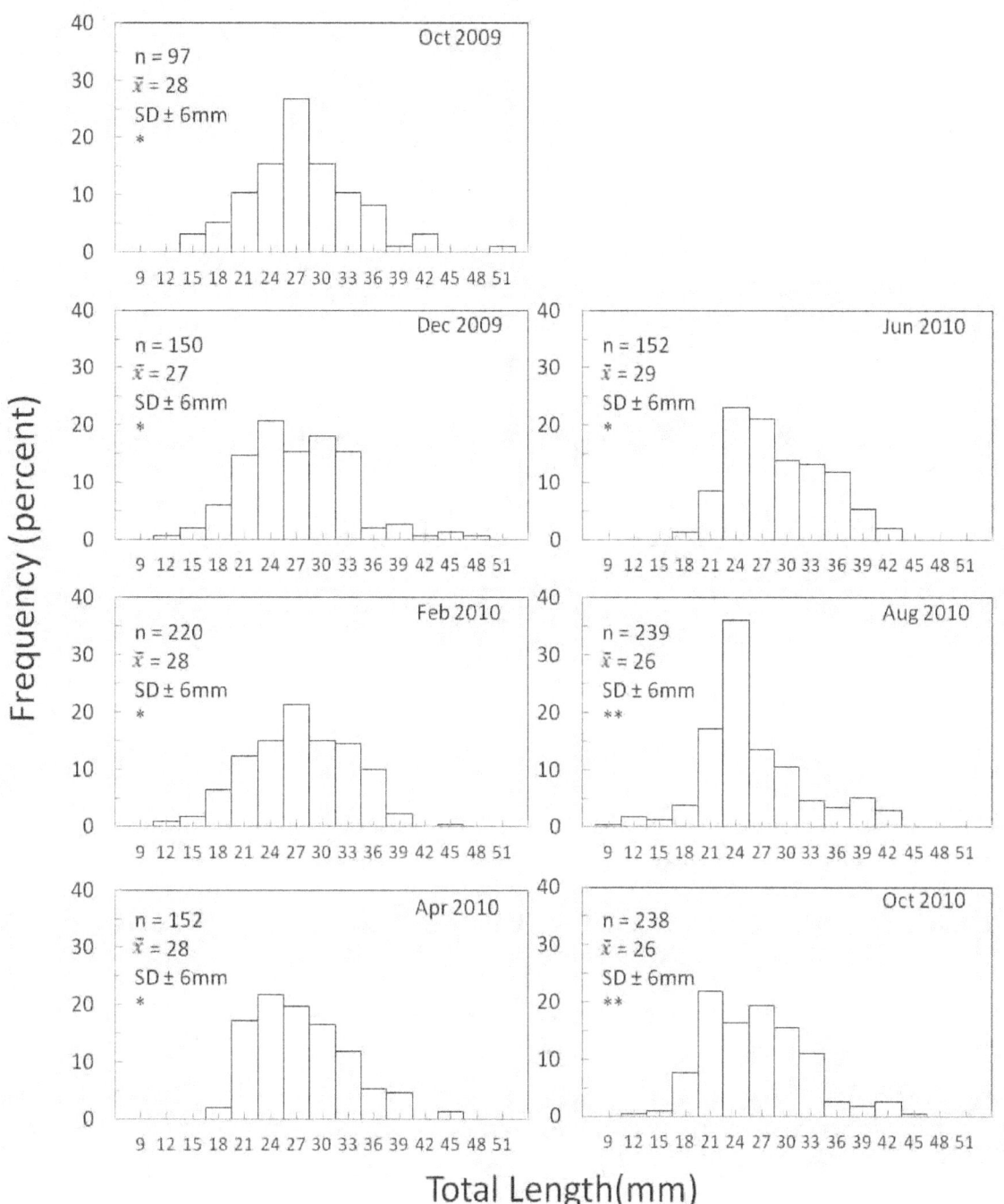

Figure 4.6. Bimonthly length-frequency distribution of Ash Meadows pupfish captured from Five Springs from October 2009 to October 2010.

Appendix

Table A.1. Seasonal food items consumed by Ash Meadows fishes and crayfish at four stations along Jackrabbit Spring system in 2009. In parenthesis is number of fish or crayfish with empty guts.

Spring 2009

Spring-pool

Species	Algae	Detritus	Plant	Substrate	Fish	Aquatic Invert	Terrestrial Invert	Unidentified Invert	Number
pupfish	93.6	2.5	0.0	0.0	0.0	3.3	0.6	0.0	8 (0)
speckled dace	0.0	0.0	0.0	5.0	0.0	45.0	50.0	0.0	2 (2)
mosquitofish	0.0	2.5	0.0	0.0	5.0	28.8	53.5	10.3	8 (0)
sailfin molly	60.0	38.3	1.7	0.0	0.0	0.0	0.0	0.0	6 (1)
crayfish	0.0	79.0	20.0	1.0	0.0	0.0	0.0	0.0	1 (1)

700-m

Species	Algae	Detritus	Plant	Substrate	Fish	Aquatic Invert	Terrestrial Invert	Unidentified Invert	Number
pupfish	96.3	1.3	0.0	0.0	0.0	2.5	0.0	0.0	8 (0)
speckled dace	0.0	0.0	0.0	0.0	0.0	7.7	57.0	35.3	3 (1)
mosquitofish	6.3	8.4	0.0	0.0	0.0	34.1	22.8	28.5	8 (0)
sailfin molly	25.0	50.0	0.0	25.0	0.0	0.0	0.0	0.0	2 (0)
crayfish	20.0	40.0	0.0	6.0	0.0	0.0	20.0	14.0	5 (4)

1800-m

Species	Algae	Detritus	Plant	Substrate	Fish	Aquatic Invert	Terrestrial Invert	Unidentified Invert	Number
pupfish	-	-	-	-	-	-	-	-	0 (0)
speckled dace	5.0	79.8	0.0	0.0	0.8	0.0	14.5	0.0	4 (0)
mosquitofish	0.0	45.3	0.0	0.0	0.0	7.3	47.5	0.0	4 (0)
sailfin molly	0.0	50.0	0.0	50.0	0.0	0.0	0.0	0.0	1 (0)
crayfish	0.0	50.0	16.7	0.0	0.0	0.0	0.0	33.3	3 (3)

3600-m

Species	Algae	Detritus	Plant	Substrate	Fish	Aquatic Invert	Terrestrial Invert	Unidentified Invert	Number
pupfish	10.0	71.0	12.6	0.0	0.0	0.1	6.3	0.0	8 (0)
speckled dace	0.0	2.5	0.0	0.0	0.0	97.5	0.0	0.0	4 (0)
mosquitofish	0.0	9.4	0.0	0.0	0.0	18.1	61.9	10.6	8 (0)
sailfin molly	-	-	-	-	-	-	-	-	0 (0)
crayfish	0.0	0.0	0.0	0.0	100.0	0.0	0.0	0.0	1 (7)

Table A.1. Seasonal food items consumed by Ash Meadows fishes and crayfish at four stations along Jackrabbit Spring system in 2009. In parenthesis is number of fish or crayfish with empty guts.—Continued

Summer 2009

Spring-pool

Species	Algae	Detritus	Plant	Substrate	Fish	Aquatic Invert	Terrestrial Invert	Unidentified Invert	Number
pupfish	94.4	3.8	0.6	1.3	0.0	0.0	0.0	0.0	8 (0)
speckled dace	37.5	0.0	6.5	0.0	6.0	12.5	37.5	0.0	2 (1)
mosquitofish	33.3	37.0	0.0	0.0	2.0	9.0	18.7	0.0	3 (1)
sailfin molly	100.0	0.0	0.0	0.0	0.0	0.0	0.0	0.0	8 (0)
crayfish	4.5	73.1	18.8	0.0	3.4	0.3	0.0	0.0	8 (0)

700-m

Species	Algae	Detritus	Plant	Substrate	Fish	Aquatic Invert	Terrestrial Invert	Unidentified Invert	Number
pupfish	96.4	0.0	0.0	0.3	2.5	0.9	0.0	0.0	8 (0)
speckled dace	19.0	31.0	0.0	0.0	0.0	0.0	50.0	0.0	2 (1)
mosquitofish	10.1	43.1	1.3	0.0	3.5	11.1	16.3	14.6	8 (0)
sailfin molly	0.0	100.0	0.0	0.0	0.0	0.0	0.0	0.0	3 (0)
crayfish	0.0	64.1	11.9	5.0	19.0	0.0	0.0	0.0	8 (0)

1800-m

Species	Algae	Detritus	Plant	Substrate	Fish	Aquatic Invert	Terrestrial Invert	Unidentified Invert	Number
pupfish	-	-	-		-	-	-	-	0 (0)
speckled dace	33.3	19.7	0.0	0.0	0.0	33.3	0.0	13.7	3 (0)
mosquitofish	0.0	32.4	0.0	0.0	0.0	2.0	36.9	28.7	7 (0)
sailfin molly	0.0	100.0	0.0	0.0	0.0	0.0	0.0	0.0	3 (0)
crayfish	33.0	67.0	0.0	0.0	0.0	0.0	0.0	0.0	1 (1)
tadpole	0.0	87.5	0.0	12.5	0.0	0.0	0.0	0.0	2 (0)

3600-m

Species	Algae	Detritus	Plant	Substrate	Fish	Aquatic Invert	Terrestrial Invert	Unidentified Invert	Number
pupfish	65.2	33.7	0.0		·0.3	0.8	0.0	0.0	6 (0)
speckled dace	0.0	66.7	0.0		33.3	0.0	0.0	0.0	3 (0)
mosquitofish	0.0	55.1	3.8		0.0	5.6	16.8	18.8	8 (0)
sailfin molly	-	-	-		-	-	-	-	0 (0)
crayfish	0.0	100.0	0.0		0.0	0.0	0.0	0.0	2 (2)

Table A.1. Seasonal food items consumed by Ash Meadows fishes and crayfish at four stations along Jackrabbit Spring system in 2009. In parenthesis is number of fish or crayfish with empty guts.—Continued

Fall 2009

Spring-pool

Species	Algae	Detritus	Plant	Substrate	Fish	Aquatic Invert	Terrestrial Invert	Unidentified Invert	Number
pupfish	82.7	0.0	0.0	13.5	2.5	0.0	0.0	1.3	8 (0)
speckled dace	0.0	50.0	0.0	0.0	0.0	50.0	0.0	0.0	2 (1)
mosquitofish	40.0	26.0	0.0	0.0	0.0	30.0	4.0	0.0	5 (3)
sailfin molly	95.8	0.0	0.0	4.2	0.0	0.0	0.0	0.0	6 (0)
crayfish	13.0	29.2	24.0	0.0	30.4	3.0	0.4	0.0	5 (0)

700-m

Species	Algae	Detritus	Plant	Substrate	Fish	Aquatic Invert	Terrestrial Invert	Unidentified Invert	Number
pupfish	57.0	0.0	1.3	35.3	2.5	4.0	0.0	0.0	4 (0)
speckled dace	26.7	33.3	3.3	0.0	3.3	33.3	0.0	0.0	3 (0)
mosquitofish	26.7	16.7	0.0	0.8	0.0	19.2	36.7	0.0	6 (0)
sailfin molly	28.8	0.0	0.0	71.3	0.0	0.0	0.0	0.0	4 (0)
crayfish	77.5	0.0	0.0	15.0	5.0	3.5	0.0	0.0	2 (0)

1800-m

Species	Algae	Detritus	Plant	Substrate	Fish	Aquatic Invert	Terrestrial Invert	Unidentified Invert	Number
pupfish	-	-	-		-	-	-	-	0 (0)
speckled dace	0.0	59.7	0.0	0.0	0.0	21.7	18.7	0.0	3 (0)
mosquitofish	0.0	40.0	0.0	0.0	0.0	29.5	13.0	17.5	2 (0)
sailfin molly	-	-	-		-	-	-	-	0 (0)
crayfish	0.0	100.0	0.0	0.0	0.0	0.0	0.0	0.0	1 (0)

3600-m

Species	Algae	Detritus	Plant	Substrate	Fish	Aquatic Invert	Terrestrial Invert	Unidentified Invert	Number
pupfish	0.0	0.0	3.8	96.3	0.0	0.0	0.0	0.0	8 (0)
speckled dace	11.0	54.3	0.0	0.0	0.0	24.0	10.7	0.0	3 (0)
mosquitofish	0.0	0.0	37.5	43.5	3.5	14.0	1.5	0.0	2 (0)
sailfin molly	0.0	0.0	0.0	100.0	0.0	0.0	0.0	0.0	3 (0)
crayfish	0.0	12.5	52.5	24.8	10.0	0.3	0.0	0.0	4 (0)

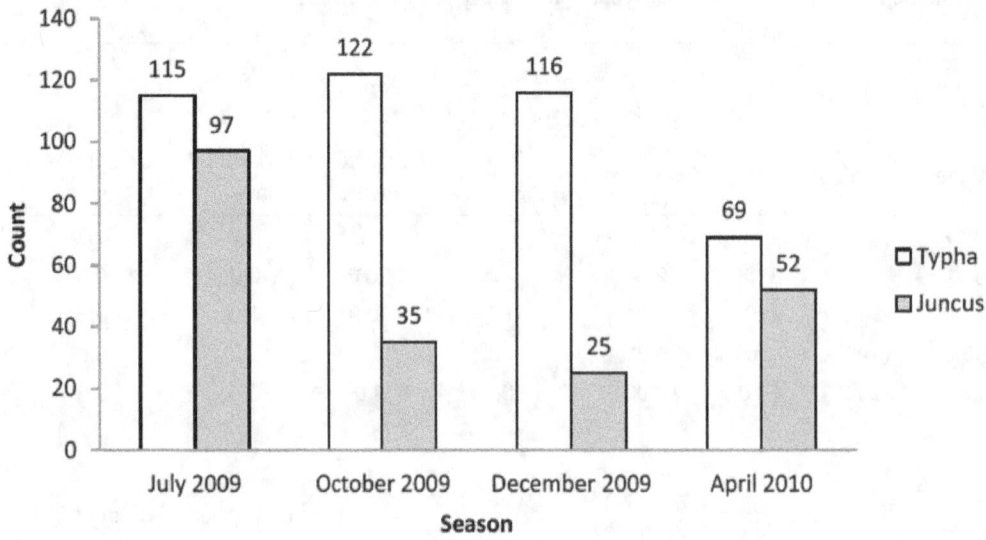

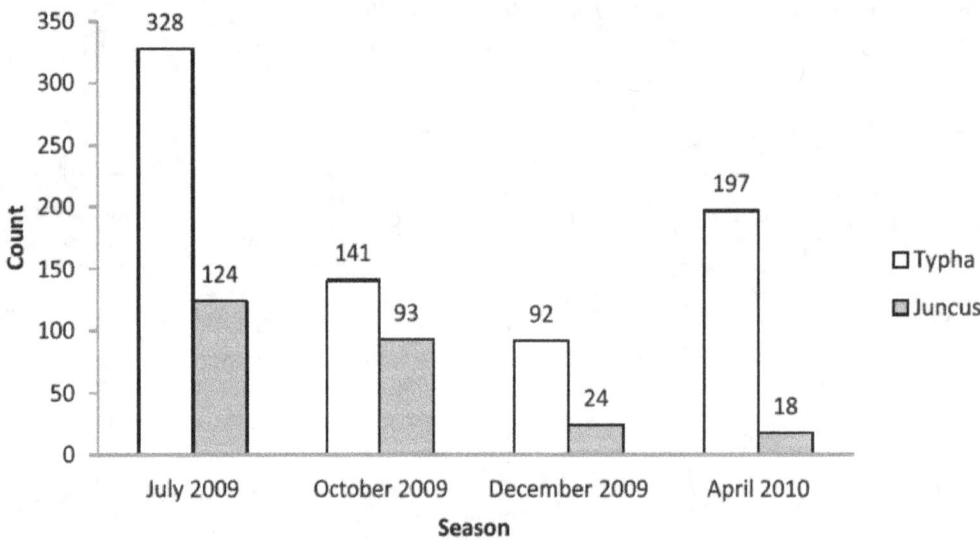

Figure A.1. Total number of western mosquitofish and red swamp crayfish from *Typha* and *Juncus* marshes in four seasons, 2009 and 2010.

www.ingramcontent.com/pod-product-compliance
Lightning Source LLC
Chambersburg PA
CBHW080438290526
45791CB00008BA/2546